Presented to:

_____

By:

_____

Date:

_____

"Words are like eyeglasses, they blur everything which they do not make more clear."   *– J. Joubert*[1]

"Think of words as instruments characterised by their use and then think of the use of a hammer, the use of a chisel, the use of a square, of a glue pot and of the glue."   *– Ludwig Wittgenstein*[2]

"I have no problem with the concept of 'language-games' as 'universes of discourse' where words are used in a particular context, but I do hold serious objections to the thesis that such universes of discourse are distinct from each other and to the relativistic idea that meaning can be wholly private and purely subjective. Words do not mean certain things because of the way in which they are used; words are used because they mean certain things. Any new or 'invented' term must be defined by pre-existing and meaningful terms."   *– Peter Williams*[3]

"I don't know what you mean by 'glory,'?" Alice said.

Humpty Dumpty smiled contemptuously. "Of course you don't — till I tell you. I meant 'there's a nice knock-down argument for you!'?"

"But 'glory' doesn't mean 'a nice knock-down argument'," Alice objected.

"When I use a word," Humpty Dumpty said, in rather a scornful tone, "it means just what I choose it to mean—neither more nor less."

"The question is," said Alice, "whether you can make words mean so many different things."

"The question is," said Humpty Dumpty, "which is to be master — that's all."

– Alice Through the Looking Glass

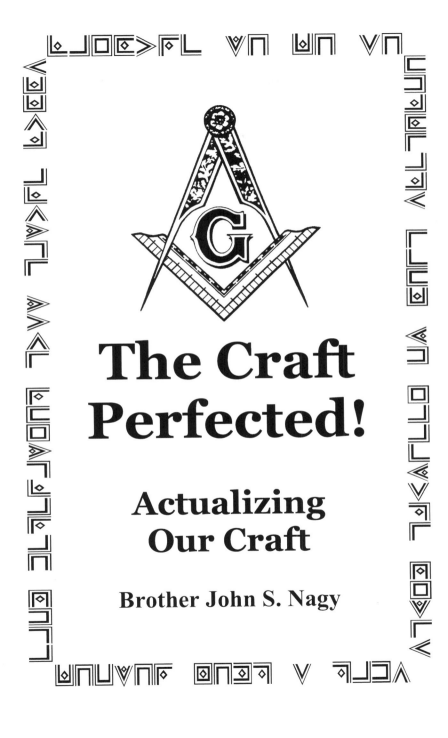

The Craft Perfected!

Actualizing Our Craft

Brother John S. Nagy

The Craft Perfected!
– Actualizing Our Craft
Copyright © 2019 Dr. John S. Nagy

Also Author of: **Building Hiram, Building Boaz, Building Athens, Building Janus, Building Perpends, Building Ruffish, Building Cement, Building Free Men, The Journeyman Papers, A Brother Asks: Vol. 1, Provoking Success,** Emotional Awareness **Made Easy**

Publisher: Promethean Genesis Publishing
PO Box 636, Lutz FL 33548-0636

ISBN-13: 978-0-9911094-5-6
First Printing, October 2019
Published in the United States of America
Book Editing, Design and Illustration
by Dr. John S. Nagy
Books available through www.coach.net

Dedication

To my Brother Builders Phil, Jeff, Art,
Nick, Kevin, & Clifford, I offer a sincere
and heartfelt *thank you* for helping to
reveal this book.

To my future Brother Builders: may this
book help Light your way as you continue
your Journey East, Perfecting Masterfully.

To my two sons: I look forward to the day
that you Embrace Maturity so that I may
gift this book to you as Men.

To my loving and supportive wife
and best friend: when you say, *"Let what
you write flow from the best parts of your
heart"*, I will, always.

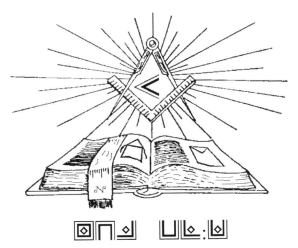

To Receive Light, One's Vessel must be Properly Prepared.

Vessels don't honor Light when they contain Vices or Superfluities. Light cannot enter well under such conditions. Even when there is room, the contents will spoil what little Light might mix with it. These burdens must be removed before Light can enter unhindered and undamaged.

Vessels must also have strength of character. They must be fully capable of holding this Light and using and projecting it inwardly, and out into the world in worthwhile ways. Manly strength must be their makeup in the form of virtues whose mere presence forces these vessels toward constructive ends.

Incomplete, uninformed and immature Vessels are unsuitable for receiving Light, much less using it for its benefits. They are by their very nature weak and unnecessarily Burdened.

They may have potential though. But to be better, they must be properly prepared to be of any good and proper use to the Builder.

Should vessels have a burning desire to receive Light Ritefully, they can do this but with little beneficial impact.

However, should they have a passion for Light, they will do what is right to receive it.

Fair & Perfect Warning

This document contains critical *Apprentice Level* connections that might cause emotions of extreme discomfort, disgust, irritation, shock, and dismay, especially if you're dead set in your preconceived notions. It's highly recommended that you read this book through to its end before you draw any rash, superficial and wholly unsupported conclusions.

Your efforts shall be rewarded!

Additionally, when it comes to Freemasonic ritual, it is always best not to discuss anything therein contained with anyone who has yet to experience it legitimately, fully, and completely. In this light, it's recommended that you not discuss in depth anything within  this book with anyone *who is not a Craft Member and who has yet to read or hear it thoroughly & completely for himself.*

There's a huge risk that you take in shallowly revealing anything in this book to others who have yet to read it through or understand it thoroughly. It may both ruin the intended experience of the book for them and prevent you from having a rich discussion with them about what it reveals.

Proceed with all due caution!

Preface

*Woe to those who read in darkness and who
imbibe in uninformed speculation; they
assume things never intended. Equally, woes
to those who listen to them intently and assume
they are informed.*

It's been said that *words mean things.* That's a
powerful statement, especially when presented with
firm convictions and evidentiary support. I loved this
notion when I first heard it. It supported a lot of what I
wanted to believe about them.

Unfortunately, as well-intended as this statement
is, when it's used to argue a word's meaning, the very
core of why the specific term is used, it falls short.
Forced interpretations typically bastardize the original
intent of a word's use.

This is the case when it comes to understanding
Freemasonic Ritual.

Freemasonic Ritual is laced with words that are at
first not understood as intended, particularly when
taken without the influence of the context of the time
it was written. Simple terms, well-understood in one
way or form today, too often have an utterly different
meaning when understood and gleaned within the
time and culture they were first offered.

Temporal Labels

It's well-known that semantic drift occurs for
some words and not others. This is where temporal
labels come in handy, especially when dealing with
dated materials. They signal to readers and listeners
when words or senses are constrained or conditioned

by times. Readers should know how words were originally used within a specific context and not just some *out of context* meanings that are commonly embraced today. It's important to know when and how they have changed or shifted their meaning.

Each temporal label denotes the meanings and senses that were assigned to the term in question within time-frames of known use for those meanings and senses. There are many such labels and below are some used for these tasks.

Dated/Old-Fashioned: Words or senses that are no longer used by the majority of English speakers but still encountered especially among a previous or older generation.

Rare/Becoming Rare: Words or senses that are rarely used or are beginning to be used less often; not in normal use.

Historical: Words or senses that are still used today, but only in reference to some practice or artifact that is no longer part of the modern world.

Archaic: Words or senses that were once common but now are rare, though they may be familiar because of their occurrence in certain contexts, such as the literature of an earlier time. More specifically, words and senses for which there is only sporadic evidence in print since 1755[4]. Also, words or senses, not in ordinary use today, though sometimes used to give a deliberately old-fashioned effect.

Obsolete: Words or senses that are no longer in active use, except, for example, in literary quotations. *Specifically, words and senses for which there is little or no printed evidence since 1755.*

Please note how each label is used to classify a word. Some have dates associated with them and others have information denoting the transition from one generational use to another. All of them let the users and researchers of such words know how the word could have been used during its history. Each label also lets users know when a term had a meaning or sense that may have been used a specific way, and potentially not another.

Ritual

Therein is the challenge faced when trying to understand Freemasonic Ritual today. Our Ritual was not written with modern understandings, meanings, and senses. Because of this, its meanings, senses and even allusions may be misunderstood and, far worse, misleading. Conveyed information not taken in the light in which it was originally offered will be filtered through lenses of modernity. As a result, Ritual terms may never hit their intended mark because filtering prevented understanding.

Terms found within our writings, like *Worshipful, Cowan, Freeborn, Free & Accepted, Free* and *Mystery,* have all shifted their meanings over the years, some more dramatically than others. Quite a few have original meanings nothing like they have today. Some of their original conveyed meaning in no way represents today's understandings. Unless the users have an in-depth understanding of their histories, their Light remains unseen and a mystery becomes known to only a few. To understand any one of these terms out of context shall bastardize what is being conveyed and focus attention in directions never intended.

Blue Lodge information is symbolic in its nature and in its delivery. This is its true untainted reality. It was and, if provided properly, is never intended to be taken literally. To benefit from its offerings, one must be properly prepared to understand its concealed meanings, a preparation that is unfortunately next to never offered in, or as, typical lodge training.

Decoding Challenges

It's not just word meanings and senses that are at issue here. Applying modern-day definitions to ritual's metaphors and allegories often bury ritual's original beautiful intents under several layers of rubbish. And who would be none the wiser for accepting this rubbish as intended when their original intents are never provided.

Complications also occur when trying to decode ritual into common day words. There are many sources that have histories and temporal labels that don't apply in one situation but do in another. More complications occur when the terms used commonly within ritual may appear to have a common sense, yet when examined through a historic lens, take on an entirely different meaning or sense. Further complications occur when terms used commonly within ritual have no modern-day equivalent.

As a result, this researcher was often left scratching his head trying to figure out a viable direction to take.

Even though these words are no longer used in a ritual provided sense in the profane world today, they are commonly used within *Ritual* in an *archaic* way in modern times. Do I label these common ritual words as *obsolete* in their use?

This does not make for easy decisions.

In the end, I came to understand that the labels do not matter for anything other than understanding that they had to be treated as special cases. These words should be understood within context. Debating *archaic* versus *obsolete* simply doesn't matter when the focus should be upon what special insight and intent is being conveyed. After much consideration, I eventually chose to convey that a word is provided within a context that has a specific sense or meaning. I believed this was enough. Doing so ended my efforts to explain things further along those lines.

Revelations

One of the many words that I've encountered within Ritual, and within older documents that explain Ritual, led me on an interesting journey of discovery. As with other words, this word was originally understood by me within the context of modern times.

As time progressed, so did my understanding of Ritual and this word. I noticed that some things simply did not fit together smoothly when this word was understood through the lens of modern meanings. I began to question the validity of many Brothers' conjectures and also the validity of many writings put forth justifying a specific view on this word.

It became clear that an investigation was in order; one that delved into both this word's understood and misunderstood uses and its historical meanings and senses. The end in mind was to ensure that the word's use was clear and that it fits neatly within that house not made with hands within every member's heart.

This writing is the result of that journey.

What I found was not only life-affirming, but life redirecting in *perfect* ways.

Definitions

Candidates – Paying patrons who play central roles within the Degrees offered by Freemasons

Craft – A skill, trade, or occupation requiring expertise; that which is produced by Craftsmen; those who engage in a Craft

Degrees – Ritual style performances enacted by Freemasons for the benefit of Candidates

Flaw – Something is missing: a mark, fault, or other characteristic that mars a substance or object; a defect, blemish, fault, weakness, or shortcoming,

Flawless – Without any blemishes, imperfections or impairments; unblemished; undamaged; error-free; unerring; pristine; impeccable; faultless; intact; ideal

Freemason – A member of the *Society of Free & Accepted Masons;* a Speculative Mason

Freemasonry – The organizational structures, principles, traditions, rules, laws, lore and rituals that support the practices of the *Society of Free & Accepted Masons*

Lodge – A group of Freemasons authorized by the *Society of Free & Accepted Masons* to enact Degrees

Mason – A Builder (of self, others, community, etc…)

Masonry – The Art and Science of Building

Perfect – Suitable for the builder's use; mature; fit; complete; whole; sane

Perfection – A state of suitability, maturity, fitness, completion, wholeness and/or sanity

Ritual – Scripted & choreographed morality-plays enacted by Freemasons for Candidates.

Stonecraft – Operative Masonry

Work – [when capitalized] Specific actions that one must engage in to improve

Words

Dated Words…
   give insights into Recent Pages.

Old-Fashioned Words…
   give insights into Nostalgic Cages[5].

Rare Words…
   give insights into Possible Sages.

Historical Words…
   give insights into Specific Ages.

Archaic Words…
   give insights into Long-Ago Stages.

But Obsolete Words…
   give insights into Long-Lost Gages[6].

Introduction

*Challenges are wholly
different from
Problems and
Troubles. Focus on the
latter two and you
miss the entire
Purpose of your
Endeavor.*

Freemasonry is facing
a huge challenge. It's been facing this challenge for
quite a few years now. It comes in the form of
messages we collectively convey as a fraternity. These
messages are not just those that we write or speak
within the lodge and without. These messages are
conveyed through our actions in every encounter and
every interaction between Brothers and others.

The messages we convey as members are
powerful too. They tell everyone who listens, directly
or indirectly, what to expect from Freemasons and
from the organization in general.

Those who listen hear us loud and clear. They let
us know what they are hearing by how we are treated
by them. No three groups speak more loudly to what
we convey than prospects, Candidates and newly
Raised members.

Prospects pay attention to who we are and what
we profess to be. They pay attention to what we have.
They look at our lifestyles and with whom and what
we surround ourselves.

Candidates pay attention too. They examine what
we have done to bring these things into being for
ourselves.

But newly Raised members pay attention to the nuts and bolts of our existence. They look at our integrity and examine whether our claims match our day to day activities, inside and outside the lodge arena.

They also draw conclusions as to whether what we do is what they want to do.

And when it's not a good match, for whatever reasons, they lose interest and leave.

Reality Check

When you want to examine the impact that messages have upon the membership, please consider the following two scenarios.

1. If you were told you could become a Master Mason by joining the Freemasonic Order, joined it and then came to find that your Brothers were indeed Masterful and who led others by Masterful example, would you want to remain a member?

I'd like to think that you would. Why wouldn't you? The very reason for which you joined was being exemplified masterfully by all those with whom you surrounded yourself. You have excellent role models from which to learn and you *know* by their example that what you want to achieve has been achieved by others.

Let's turn this situation around.

2. If you were told you could become a Master Mason by joining the Freemasonic Order, joined it and then came to find that not one of your Brothers thought himself Masterful much less led

others by Masterful example, would you want to remain a member?

I'd hazard a guess that you wouldn't stick around for very long. Why would you? The reality you're facing is disappointing. The very reason you joined isn't exemplified by any member before you. Moreover, your teachers don't actually believe Mastery is possible in any one's lifetime. You don't have any role models from which to learn. You don't know for sure that what you wanted to achieve has been achieved by anyone with whom you have before you.

This last situation contrasts the first purposefully. It contains overwhelming messages that greet many Candidates after they have reached the level of Master Mason. It's discouraging, depressing and it's unsupportive of their goals.

Empowering Messages

The messages we give to our members should be ones of hope. They should be ones that say that what we espouse is achievable, doable within one's lifetime, *and doable early enough in one's Masonic career to enjoy the fruit of such achievement.* These messages should not be ones of dogmatic lip service either. They should be shown through our membership's daily habits and achievements outside the confines of our lodge's walls.

On the contrary, any message provided by our members that conveys that what we espouse is achievable *only in death* is one that is counter-productive to our ends. Furthermore, it conveys despairingly that the Mastery we hold in such high regard is never going to occur for anyone to enjoy in his lifetime.

Messages that convey and assure that Mastery is both desirable and achievable long before death is a message that motivates and holds the attention of those who wish to obtain this for themselves.

Messages surrounding us and conveying evidence that Masters have existed since time immemorial adds to this motivation. Messages about achieved Mastery backed by present-day evidence are even more powerful, especially when presented in the form of successful members who are part of the very lodge to which aspirants wish to belong.

Perfect Clarity

It became clear to me that this book needed to be written. This clarity came during a prompting phone conversation with a Brother who lived on the other side of our North American continent. Like so many other conversations, we had an initial specific topic of focus. Once it was addressed, we wandered in many other directions.

The topic we eventually wandered into was the unanticipated impact that an interesting piece of information had upon members and, more specifically, upon the old-timers who had been in the fraternity for several decades.

Why would this piece of information be the focus of our conversation? Why would it have an impact that was so unanticipated that it would warrant writing an entire book? But most of all, how could any such book be so different from other efforts put forth in writing by a diligent student of Masonry that it warranted being written at all?

What was that important piece of information?

As you might have already guessed by the book's title, it has to do with the word *perfect.* And more specifically, it was the definition of this word as applied toward Masonic Work.

Sadly, the definition that's presently being conveyed is in the form of a strong counterproductive message. It's one that is exemplified by the attitudes and behaviors of our current members. Unfortunately, it also discourages hope of Mastery in one's lifetime.

If there is any hope for a more empowering message, then we as a fraternity need to get on the same page as to what we convey to both members and profanes alike.

Herein is a radically different message; *one of hope, empowerment, and achievement!*

Its focus is upon a view of this word *perfect* as it's used within our Freemasonic Ritual and instruction, how it has been usurped by well-meaning contemporary zealots to undermine the intended message of our progenitors and the Work focus that helps bring it forth from within our members.

But most of all, it's a message that should have been conveyed uninterrupted and undistorted by our members from our beginnings.

When you consider...

- What we're supposed to be doing as lodges
- What we're supposed to be producing as lodges
- What purpose our doing and producing is actually serving in this world

Then you might better understand the message *we should be carrying* as we engage our members in all these activities.

Perhaps, after you have read this work, you'll be better prepared to carry this well-understood message in every manner and form as you engage yourself inside and outside the lodge, into the future.

I. The Perfect Problem

The root of the word "problem" alludes to obstacles that are thrown forth in one's path. At the heart of every problem is something that is in the way.

It was about fourteen years into my membership that I finally tried to explore in depth this thing called *The Perfect Ashlar.* Admittedly, my quest  had an agenda. Too often I heard one learned Brother after another use the term expressed with an abundantly clear attitude that *no one could become* this *Perfect Ashlar.*

This raised serious questions within my soul as to whether such opinions were counterproductive to both our fraternity and our members. When queried about the basis behind such comments it became obvious their comments were more based on misunderstood religious scriptures than actual Masonic reality. They didn't realize this since most of them had only repeated back what was *repeated back to them.*

This was typical of our fraternity. Members are provided only partial light at best and even this was either grossly misunderstood or poorly misrepresented by those conveying it. Substance was ignored in favor of form and as long as it had the appearance desired by the judging parties, it was deemed suitable.

Unfortunately, the judging parties were almost always misinformed and superficial in their understanding of things that required in-depth knowledge and understanding to be conveyed appropriately.

Premises

Those opinions put forth were based upon premises long-established by individuals steeped in their personal beliefs. They linger on lips even now conveying lore as writ to members having never been examined, much less investigated.

Was the word *perfect* conveying what they claimed? Were their premises correct? Did they use it within the context of Speculation consistent and supportive of its Operative roots? How did we know that what they preached was in the true spirit of Operative craft practiced speculatively? The questions poured forth unendingly.

After hearing these conjectures *ad nauseum,* I was pulled toward another agenda. What was needed was a clear and concise investigation into the term *Perfect Ashlar* for further Light to be shared properly with the Craft. This meant in-depth research that few would have the courage to undertake.

As much as I had explored this term up to now, I had never dared ask some of the more intriguing questions or to question the assumptions of my earlier efforts. Admittedly, in my earlier efforts, I had been too swept away by a tsunami of previously read Freemasonic works to focus on something seemingly trivial as an all too familiar symbol. As a result of this unanticipated condition, I had missed some very important Light.

And therein lay the problem – false assumptions! And it was a perfect problem to have!

Realizing this, I was soon carried away by another wave of investigation. I began by exploring where the term *Perfect Ashlar* first appeared. I truly thought that it would be a simple thing to discover since the term was so abundantly sprinkled throughout Freemasonic literature and Ritual. I thought a symbol like this would have a clear trail of existence that would reach way back into the very first writings available. I was rapidly to find out that in these thoughts I was mistaken.

The Missing Trail

I expected it would be a simple enough task to do. I believed that all I needed to complete it were the old manuscripts, digitized *optical character recognized* versions of the old charges of course, and an adequate search engine. I initially conceived that by plugging in the term *Perfect Ashlar* I would see a splattering of search term hits scattered before me as rice at a wedding exit.

As you could imagine, to my chagrin, this did not occur. In fact, the more I plugged away at my efforts, the shorter I came up in my results. I even tried variations on the term. I left the word *ashlar* out and did many searches through many Stonecraft related documents just using the word *perfect*. I then tried searching using just *ashlar* and didn't find one instance remotely connected with what I sought. No matter what archaic writing I encountered, the term *Perfect Ashlar* remained startlingly absent!

I stopped searching the old manuscripts soon thereafter and refocused upon documents that came out during the eighteenth century. My figuring was that, if such a term was to be found, it would be easily seen in documents that came out during a century where Freemasonry was in its infancy. After all, the term is widely used today as part and parcel of an admirable but unattainable end-in-mind that many members espouse. Surely it would have been present from the beginning!

As fate would have it, I was unable to identify one single document that contained the term. In fact, not only did I not come across the term in any of these documents, my research network reported the same findings. There simply was no evidence to be found through my typical research channels.

It was only toward the end of my research project that I came across something that I had stuffed into my *look into later* folder. It was an entry in Brother Mackey's 1916 edition of his well-known encyclopedia.

> **Ashlar** - *This is defined by Bailey as "Freestone[7] as it comes out of the quarry." In speculative Freemasonry, we adopt the ashlar, in two different states, as symbols in the Apprentice's Degree. The Rough Ashlar, or stone in its rude and unpolished condition, is emblematic of man in his natural state---*

*ignorant, uncultivated, and vicious. But when
education has exerted its wholesome influence
in expanding his intellect, restraining his
passions, and purifying his life, he then is
represented by the Perfect Ashlar, which,
under the skillful hands of the workmen, has
been smoothed, and squared, and fitted for its
place in the building. In the older lectures of
the eighteenth century the Perfect Ashlar is not
mentioned, but its place was supplied by the
Broached Thurnel.*

It was the last line that confirmed for me that my research into this topic and issue was correct. Brother Mackey's entry confirmed for me that the *Perfect Ashlar* was an innovation to ritual and that it likely occurred along a timeline that had a trail of evidence that could be revealed.

This left me, and now others who have read this, with the driving question needing to be answered: *When exactly did the Perfect Ashlar enter into Freemasonic Lexicon?*

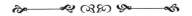

Points to Perpend:

1) What research efforts have you tried?
2) Which methods did you employ successfully?
3) What successes can you share?
4) Knowing what you know now, how would you have done things differently?

II. The Ashlar Hunt

When in doubt, seek to become well-informed!

Soon after I raised the question as to when the *Perfect Ashlar* term first entered into the Freemasonic lexicon, I found myself questioning other things. One of the questions had to do with the word *ashlar*. What exactly is it from the viewpoint of operative masons? How did it come into their use and did it come from other sources before it was adopted into Stonecraft lexicon?

My queries were not answered quickly. However, insights did come forth slowly as I explored further.

Ashlar

The first insight came to me after I asked, "Why use the word *ashlar* at all?" It's a good question to ask, especially if you're a Builder.

The word, *ashlar,* came into use during the 14th century. At that time it meant, "square stone for building or paving". It came from the Old French word, "aiseler; aisselier" meaning, *crossbeam*" (from "ais", meaning, *board),* which itself came from the Latin word, *axillaris.* This word, in turn, came from the Latin word, *axilla,* which is diminutive of *axis,* meaning "board, plank"[8].

The stone sense applied to this word is peculiar to English. Interestingly enough, the word is also used in carpentry and denotes "a short stud between joists and sloping rafters, especially near the eaves"[9].

Stonecrafters, in their efforts to build with stone, inevitably found that shaping it into board or plank-like forms made construction easier with far better results when bonding agents were applied to hold these stones together.

The use of the word was a natural segue in a building trade whose members likely rubbed close shoulders with those who used different materials in their craft. The word *ashlar* came into use within Stonecraft as a suitable metaphor for like materials used in others trades.

As with many things within Freemasonic lexicon, the use of Stonecraft terms as references for the props used within its rituals is no exception. The term *ashlar* is used specifically to refer to two items revealed within the first degree and are indicative of Candidate transition should the Candidate invest himself in doing Masonic Work.

That Work will be discussed later in favor of a more pressing issue:

When did ashlars first enter into Freemasonic ritual?

Speculative Roots

I thought it would be a valuable exercise to examine how the Perfect Ashlar had been expressed in published Rituals over the years. I figured it might lend great support to my understanding of the symbol. The more I researched, the more I encountered information relating perfection to definitions other than *flawlessness* that are typically conveyed by the majority of the membership. This became increasingly evident to me as I poked and combed through three hundred years of published Rituals, once I included non-Freemasonic sources. By doing so, the trends which these rituals revealed were quite interesting.

Initially, I believed Masonic ritual would be the best resource for the topic. I was mistaken. I had not anticipated what I would find, and I am grateful that I didn't limit my searches to what was offered by Freemasonic authors alone. As I started my investigation, I went to my usual United States Masonic ritual sources. I found that most of the openly available resources dating from the early part of the nineteenth century onward have mentions of the Perfect Ashlar.

Origins

The first published mention of the perfect ashlar appears to have occurred in the 1812 version of Thomas Webb's Freemason Monitor.[10] The exact wording, as reported by W. C. Prime, is as follows:

"The movable and immovable jewels also claim our attention in this section. They are the rough ashlar, perfect ashlar and Trestle board..."

Unfortunately, this is only what is reported since I was unable to secure an 1812 edition of this book to see the written words myself. However, in the 1818 version, which I do have, this is what appears:

"The movable and immovable jewels also claim our attention in this section. The rough ashlar is a stone as taken from the quarry in its rude and natural state. The perfect ashlar is

a stone made ready by the hands of the workman to be adjusted[11] by the tools of the fellow craft."

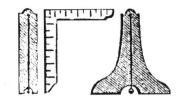

I noticed that the mention of the Perfect Ashlar was always associated with being part of the *jewels.* Curiously, there is no mention of the actual jewels in the 1797 version of Thomas Webb's Monitor. This version of his monitor is very different from those of his that were published thereafter.

Earlier Published Ritual

Throughout Freemasonry in most of the USA, you shall see in one form or another, the following words (blatantly found spelled out in "monitors" and therefore not a secret):

> *"The rough ashlar is a stone as taken from the quarry in its rude and natural state. The perfect ashlar is a stone made ready by the hands of the workmen to be adjusted by the Fellow-Craft."*

These two sentences, or something very similar to them, are provided to Candidates almost everywhere within the United States. This description of the jewels has not always been this way.

There was another reported Freemasonic manuscript that was discovered in 1730, a mere five years after the first reported production of the now well known Hiram Abiff tale, which is taken to be from 1696. Its text is as follows:

Q: Are there any jewells in your lodge?
A: Yes three, Perpend Esler a Square
pavement and a broad ovall [12]

This is the first written public document of what is interpreted to be a word indicating an ashlar (Eslar), and a perpend stone at that, is one of the jewels (jewells) of the lodge.

Four years later in 1700, we see within another public document jewels that somewhat echoed the 1696 document. The text is as follows:

Q. - Are there any Jewells in your Lodge?
A. - Three, Perpendester, a Square pavement
and a Broked-mall [13]

Within that same year, another public document had only one of the three jewels somewhat the same as the other document published that year. Its text is as follows:

Q. - How many Jewles belong to your Lodge?
A. - There are three the Square pavemt the
blazing Star and the Danty tassley. [14]

It would be fourteen years later in 1714 that the Perpend Ashlar would reappear in another public document, along with the square pavement present in the 1696 version. The text is as follows:

Q. - Are there any Jewells in your Lodge?
A. - Three, a Perpendester a Square Pavement
& a covered Kinall [15]

It is interesting to note that in a manuscript[16] published in 1724, only ten years later, we have an entirely different set of Jewels that are introduced into the fold. They are referred to as *precious jewels* and its text is as follows:

> *Q. How many precious Jewels?*
> *A. Three; a square Asher, a Diamond, and a Square.*
> *Q. What do they represent?*
> *A. The Three Persons, Father, Son, and Holy Ghost*

Currently, there exist *precious jewels* within some Rituals. However, they are nothing like what is written in this 1724 manuscript.

Three years later, in 1727, another manuscript[17] shows that the jewels in question are now referred to as *Immovable*. This may have been to differentiate them from the *precious jewels* that had made their way into ritual as indicated by the 1724 document.

The newly labeled jewels are incorporated into a more elaborate and purposeful catechism. The text is as follows:

> *Q. - Have you any Immoveable Jewels in Yr Lodge?*
> *A. - We have.*
> *Q. - How many?*
> *A. - Three.*
> *Q. - What are they?*
> *A. - The Mosaick Pavement, the dented Asler & the broach Urnell.*
> *Q. - What's the first Use of them?*

A. - The Mosaick Pavement for the Master to draw his design upon; the dented Asler for the fellow Craft to try their Iewells on; And the broach Urnell for the Entered Apprentice to Work upon.

In 1730, in just three more years, the continuation of the use of the term *immovable jewels* is well-established and the introduction of the rough ashlar as a jewel is firmly established within ritual that is known to the public. Its text is as follows:

Q. - What are the Immoveable Jewels?
A. - Trasel Board, Rough Ashler, and Broach'd Thurnel.
Q. - What are their Uses?
A. - Trasel Board for the Master to draw his Designs upon, Rough Ashler for the Fellow-Craft to try their Jewels upon, and the Broach'd Thurnel for the Enter'd 'Prentice to learn to work upon.[18]

In 1745, fifteen years later, a French publication, "*Catechisme Des Francs-Maçons*", refers to the rough ashlar as *the crude stone*. It does its best to describe another stone as well and continues the use of a drawing board. Here is the text:

D. Qui sont les trois immuables?
R. La Pierre brute pour les Apprentifs, la Pierre cubique à pointe, pour aiguiser les outils des, Compagnons, & la Planche à tracer fur laquelle les Maîtres font leurs deiïèins.[19]

I'm informed that these lines translate from French to English as follows:

> *Q. What are the three immovable?*
> *A. The crude stone for the Apprentices, the*
> *   cubic pointed stone, to sharpen the tools*
> *   for, Fellows, and the drawing board, upon*
> *   which the Masters make their plans.*

Brother William Preston, twenty-seven years later, in 1772 continues the use of the rough ashlar and drawing board but makes yet another change. He refers to the other stone as a smooth one. The text is as follows:

> *Q. Name the immoveable Jewels.*
> *A. The rough ashlar, smooth ashlar and the*
> *   tracing board.*[20]

By the next time we see another publication of ritual containing the immovable jewels, it is, as was mentioned earlier, within "*Thomas Webb's Monitor*" and, with very little deviation (such as, referring to them as *movable* or *immovable*, depending upon the jurisdiction), it has remained consistent thereafter.

Thereafter

Reviewing how the use of the term *ashlar* unfolded over time, it is clear that it was in various forms integrated into ritual early on during the Premier Grand Lodge era. The insertion and transformation of *jewels* within the Ritual, in their varying configurations, occurred within the following one hundred years. The original perpend ashlar, the stone which would likely be a dimensional stone whose height was much shorter in dimension than its width and lengths, was to transform into a perfect ashlar whose three dimensions were of equal value with smooth surfaces all around.

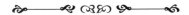

Jewel Evolution since 1696

Year	Jewel	Jewel	Jewel	Source
1696	Broad Ovall	Perpend Esler	Square Pavement	Edinburgh Register House MS
1700	The Blazing Star	The Danty Tassley.	The Square Pavement	Chetwode Crawley MS
1700	Broked-Mall	Perpendester	Square Pavement	Sloane No.3329 MS
1714	Covered Kinall	Perpendester	Square Pavement	The Kevan MS
1724	Square Asher	Diamond	Square	The Grand Mystery
1727	The Dented Asler	The Broach Urnell	The Mosaick Pavement	The Grand Mystery (1724)
1730	Rough Asher	Broach'd Thurnel	Trasel Board	Masonry Dissected
1745	The Crude Stone	The Cubic Pointed Stone	The Drawing Board	Catechisme Des Francs-Maçons
1772	The Rough Ashlar	The Smooth Ashlar Or Polished Ashlar	The Tracing Board	William Preston; 1st Degree Lecture
1812	The Rough Ashlar	The Perfect Ashlar	The Trestle Board	Thomas Webb's Monitor

III. A Cubic Reality

In this quest to find further light, I went back to the French documents that referred to one of the jewels as a *cubic pointed stone*. The two French Rituals came into England in 1744 and 1745. I found it interesting how the

> **Cubic** (adj.):
> …
> *[Mathematics]*
> *of or Relating*
> *to the Third*
> *Degree.*

translation of the Ritual brought about a description that begged for investigation.

My first stop was Brother Mackey's Encyclopedia. It had the following information:

> **Cubical Stone:** This symbol is called *pierre cubique* by the French Masons, and *cubik stein* by the German Masons. It is the Perfect Ashlar of the English and American rites.

Not wanting to take anything for granted, I looked up what a *cubic stone* was within a glossary found at a modern-day stone mason's website.

> **Cubic Stone**: *Dimension units more than 2 inches thick, e.g., cubic limestone, cubic marble.*[21]

To my surprise, there was no mention of any of the sides being equal in dimension. It was simply a straightforward description, "*Dimension units more than 2 inches thick*".

I did not want to presuppose anything about the dimensions though. Because of the culture that most people grow up within today, including myself, they would never have imagined that a cube could be anything other than a six equal sided die shaped figure. Much like the terms *perfect square* and *oblong square* have been replaced with the present day *square* and *rectangle* respectively, I knew the term *cubic stone* would need to be understood within the context of the time to which it was first used and the culture using it.

Granted, I could have easily just brushed it off and not explored this any further. But since I started exploring the use of this term within the Stonecraft world, I soon became aware of distinct differences in meaning.

It was an interesting sojourn too, since I found myself a bit shocked when I first came across descriptions that were counter to everything I had come to know.

Traction

The first indication that I was to experience a paradigm shift was when I encountered two different terms with definitions that were antagonistic to what I thought I knew. Both came from a glossary of terms used within the modern Stonecraft world. Those terms were Cubic Limestone and Cubic Marble, which I found by looking up *cubic stone*. The terms were defined as stated below:

1. **Cubic Limestone:** Dimension units more than two inches thick.[22]
2. **Cubic Marble:** Fabricated dimensional marble units more than two inches in thickness.[23]

These definitions led me to look up the first term to see how it was being used in sentences by Stonecrafters. As luck would have it, I encountered a modern book on stone work that had this sentence offered as an example:

"Coincidentally, at the time of construction, sawn cubic limestone - three-feet-eight inches by two-feet-six inches by fourteen inches - proved economical as a structural bearing wall for these buildings."[24]

Upon reading it I had instant confusion. I asked myself, "How could *cubic stone* measurements have differing dimensions?" I was perplexed by what I read. It simply didn't fit into my understanding of how the word *"cubic" should* be used. To defend my already entrenched understanding, I figured that it must be an irregular use of the word, so I endeavored to see if the Stonecraft industry terms were universally understood within it.

I was surprised by what I found in many Stonecraft books. One of them had the following:

"The bricks of the Greeks were commonly cubical and of different sizes. One size was a foot on all sides, another kind fifteen inches; the former was chiefly used in the construction of private, and the latter in public edifices. There was a third kind, a foot square and six inches thick, and a fourth kind, fifteen inches square and seven and a half inches thick; these last two kinds were called half bricks, and were used for the purpose of better effecting the construction of a bond."[25]

The last two types were of most interest to me. *It was clear that all these forms were not dimensioned where all sides were equal.* Yet, these last types were still considered *cubical as well.*

This confirmed for me that within the operative Stonecraft, cubic and cubical forms *did not* necessarily mean all sides were equal.

It was later on within that same book that yet another twist was provided to me. I read the following:

"The two stones as hollowed out are shown at Nos. 3 and 4. To show how they are wrought, we will commence with one of the stones after being brought to the cubical form. Let this stone be No. 3." [26]

The reference to No. 3 was soon followed by:

"Nos. 1, 2, 3, exhibit the first, second, and third stones of the niche as if wrought to the form of the spherical surface; No. 3 being the keystone; therefore the two remaining stones are wrought in a reverse order to the stones exhibited at No. 1 and No. 2." [27]

As clearly stated within the description, the cubical form denoted by No. 3 was a keystone and not a rectangular stone. This essentially meant that a cubical form was *any three dimensional stone with no dimension being less than two inches*, not just those that conform to shapes containing ninety-degree angles at all vertices.

Going back to the French ritual reference to the cubical pointed stone, (la Pierre cubique à pointe), it's clear that the stone in question was a three dimensional stone that was shaped toward a purpose that was suitable for sharpening Fellow Craft tools. Furthermore, it is also clear that this stone was not anywhere near what most Freemasons today would refer to as a *cubical stone*, much less a *perfect ashlar*.

Further corroboration on much of my findings was discovered within Brother Mackey's later editions to his encyclopedia. Indicating information had come forth since earlier publications, he (or his book's editors) added the following entry:

ASHLAR, PERFECT

The publication of a number of Minute Books of old Lodges since it was written calls for a revision of the paragraph on ASHLAR, on page 107. In one of his memoranda on the building of St. Paul's, Sir Christopher Wren shows by the context that as the word was there and then used an ashlar was a stone, ready-dressed from the quarries (costing about $5.00 in our money), for use in walls; and that a "perpend asheler" was one with polished ends each of which would lie in a surface of the wall; in that case a "rough" ashlar was not a formless mass of rock, but was a stone ready for use, no surface of which would appear in the building walls; it was unfinished in the sense of unpolished. In other records, of which only a few have been found, a "perpend" ashlar was of stone cut with a key in it so as to interlock with a second stone cut correspondingly.

It is doubtful if the Symbolic Ashlars were widely used among the earliest Lodges; on the other hand they are mentioned in Lodge inventories often enough to make it certain that at least a few of the old Lodges used them; and since records were so meagerly kept it is possible that their use may have been more common than has been believed. On April 11, 1754, Old Dundee Lodge in Wapping, London, "Resolved that A New Perpend Ashlar Inlaid with Devices of Masonry Valued at £2 12s. 6d. be purchased." The word "new" proves that the Lodge had used an Ashlar before 1754, perhaps for many years before; the word "devices" suggests long years of symbolic use.

It is obvious that the Ashlars as referred to in the above were not like our own Perfect and Imperfect Ashlars. It is certain that our use of them did not originate in America; there are no known data to show when or where they originated, but it is reasonable to suppose that Webb received them from Preston, or else from English Brethren in person who knew the Work in Preston's period. Operative Masons doubtless used the word in more than one sense, depending on time and place; and no rule can be based on their Practice.

The Speculative Masons after 1717, as shown above, must have used "Perfect Ashlar" in the sense of "Perpend Ashlar"; nevertheless the general purpose of the symbolism has been the same throughout - a reminder to the Candidate that he is to think of himself as if he were a building stone and that he will be expected to polish himself in manners and character in order to find a place in the finished Work of Masonry. The contrast between the Rough Ashlar and the Perfect Ashlar is not as between one man and another man, thereby generating a snobbish sense of superiority; but as between what a man is at one stage of his own self-development and what he is at another stage.

In Sir Christopher Wren's use of "ashlar" (he was a member of Lodge of Antiquity) the stone had a dimension of 1 x 1 x 2 feet; and many building records, some of them very old, mention similar dimensions; certainly, the "perpend" or "perfect" ashlar almost never was a cube, because there are few places in a wall where a cube will serve. Because in our own symbolism the Perfect Ashlar is a cube, a number of commentators on symbolism have drawn out of it pages of speculation on the properties of the cube, and on esoteric meanings they believe those properties to possess; the weight possessed by those theorizings is proportionate to the knowledge and intelligence of the commentator; but in any event these cubic interpretations do not have the authority of Masonic history behind them.

NOTE. During the many years of building and re-building at Westminster Abbey the clerk of the works kept a detailed account of money expended, money received, wages, etc. These records, still in existence, are called Fabric Rolls. In the Fabric Roll for 1253 the word "asselers" occurs many times, and means dressed stones, or ashlars. A "perpens" or "parpens," or "perpent-stone" was "a through stone," presumably because it was so cut that each end was flush with a face of the wall. It proves that "perpend ashlar" was not a "perfect ashlar" in the present sense of being a cube.

The key passages from above are as follows:

1. It is doubtful if the *Symbolic Ashlars* were widely used among the earliest Lodges.
2. It is obvious that the Ashlars referred to in the above excerpt were not like our own *Perfect* and *Imperfect Ashlars*.
3. Operative Masons doubtless used the word [perfect] in more than one sense, depending on time and place; *and no rule can be based on their Practice.*
4. The Speculative Masons after 1717, as shown above, must have used *Perfect Ashlar* in the sense of *Perpend Ashlar*.
5. The contrast between the *Rough Ashlar* and the *Perfect Ashlar* is ... ... between what a man is at one stage of his own self-development and what he is at another stage.
6. ...the stone had a dimension of 1 x 1 x 2 feet; and many building records, some of them very old, mention similar dimensions; certainly, the *perpend* or *perfect ashlar* almost never was a cube, because there are few places in a wall where a cube will serve...
7. ...our own symbolism the *Perfect Ashlar* is a cube...these cubic interpretations do not have the authority of Masonic history behind them.
8. A *perpens* or *parpens* or *perpent-stone* was *a through stone*, presumably because it was so cut that each end was flush with a face of the wall. It proves that *perpend ashlar* was not a *perfect ashlar* in the present sense of being a cube.

The key points reinforced by these passages are as follows:

1. *Symbolic Ashlars* (rough & perfect) *were not certainly widely used early on.*
2. These ashlars *were unlike those currently used.*
3. Operatives used the word *perfect* in more than one sense *and the rules for use are questionable.*
4. Speculative Masons used the term *perfect ashlar* in the sense of a *perpend ashlar* after 1717.
5. Cubic interpretations by speculative Craft commentators (and authors) are *not supported by Stonecraft history.*
6. Ashlars contrasted *stages of self-development.*

Although I was excited by all these finds, at this point my head was spinning. The symbolic ashlars were likely not widely used early on. They were not like the ones we use today. The term *perfect* had more than one meaning. Our speculative Brothers took liberty in their renaming the perpend ashlar used by our operative Brothers. The only one seemingly sure thing was that the symbolic ashlars represented contrasting stages of self-development.

I found myself questioning many things I thought I knew about ritual and our supposed history that I was told had gone unchanged since time-immemorial! Why did these things change? Why were there obvious innovations? *Why are we told things that are simply not true?*

I also found myself compelled to find the missing keys that would explain all this and do so without any benefit of a doubt.

IV. The Smooth Operators

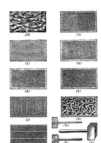

Appearance is often times not what it might seem to be nor as practical as one might have concluded.

It was not long after I had encountered the smooth ashlar denoted within Brother Preston's lectures that I had a question arise within me as to this specific finish. *Were all perfect ashlar stone finishes smooth?* This was an item previously encountered that required some deeper exploring.

I knew the question didn't make sense because it was clear from the research that the *perfect ashlar* was introduced into Ritual several years after the occurrence of Brother Preston's first mention of the smooth ashlar.

But it didn't matter if my question didn't follow a linear timeline. The question was raised and had to be responded to and with due respect to the issues at hand.

I thereafter began exploring ashlar surfaces. This was spurred on by a series of in-depth conversations that I had with well-informed Brothers and what Brother Mackey reported about the *"few places in a wall where a cube will serve"*.

It came to light that some of us had experience in the real world. We absolutely questioned the viability of a smooth surface being practical for building purposes.

As a result, the topics of these discourses were all focusing on the suitability of any structure using smooth surfaces in their building blocks coupled with a clear understanding that a smooth surface lacked the texture required for cement to properly bond.

The conversations were quite revealing!

Viability

Without question, a polished stone surface does not hold on to cement. You can apply that cement under the most ideal conditions and it still will not adhere. Once it cures, the hardened material will hold the shape of the polished surface but not the surface itself. With very little effort, cured cement lifts off a smooth surface.

This is because cement needs a textured surface to grab hold of to keep it from moving; much like a jigsaw puzzle piece must be locked into place to prevent its movement.

To smooth any surface beyond a specific point that is intended to be covered with cement is counter-productive. It simply doesn't promote good bonds when two or more surfaces are being cemented together.

When it comes to cementing stones together, surface texture is important. It is only exposed surfaces that do not have cement upon them that need to be worked differently. That difference may entail smoothing, but more likely, it is to be in line with what type of appearance the builder is asked to produce.

"Wait!" you may exclaim in protest due to some preconceived notion that the surfaces of ashlars must be smooth to be *perfect*. And you might likely have thought this if you had not said it out loud, especially if you have not actually worked in construction.

The fact is there are at least twenty-seven different surface types, all called *finishes,* which Stonecrafters use when bringing any ashlar into a usable *perfect* state.

Each finished surface has a specific purpose and function. Each finish can be used in combination with others. It all depends upon what effect the builder is required to render in the final structure.

Here is a list of some of the many finishes that can be used upon the surfaces of ashlars:

- Axed finish
- Boasted finish
- Brushed finish
- Cobbled finish
- Combed finish
- Circular finish
- Chisel-Draughted finish
- Flamed finish
- Furrowed finish
- Hammer Dressed finish
- Honed finish
- Margin finish
- Molded finish
- Natural finish
- Plain finish
- Polished finish
- Punched finish
- Quarry Faced finish
- Reticulated finish
- Rubbed finish
- Sandblasted finish
- Scrabbling finish
- Sunk finish
- Thermal finish
- Tooled finish
- Tumbled finish
- Vermiculated finish

The one in question, the *Smooth* or *Polished* finish, had its proper place only when the design of the building required it and when the surface was exposed and not joined to other surfaces. Otherwise, the use of this surface was useless for building purposes. This is key to what must be considered as you transform yourself using the Freemasonic paradigm.

The Symbolic Blue Lodge is speculative in its nature. The Smooth Ashlar is symbolic of transforming yourself from a rough to the desired finish. That end finish denoted by the Blue Lodge paradigm has nothing to do with smoothness. *It has to do with the Work you put in to transform yourself toward what the Degree directs you to do.*

V. Be Thee Perfect

*"Most of the disputes in the world arise
from words." -- Lord Mansfield* [28]

As with many
research projects,
it's often the last
effort one puts
forth that yields
the most

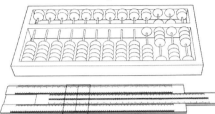

rewarding insights. This research project was no
exception to this pattern. Only toward the end of this
project was a semantic gem noticed that was there all
along yet remained unnoticed due to a diverted focus
of this effort.

While combing through definitions for the word
perfect from various sources, there was one definition
that continued to show itself that was previously
ignored. Denoted as *obsolete,* it was in almost every
search result in one form or another. Yet unexamined,
it remained as a subtle reminder of another rabbit hole
that went uninvestigated. Being frank about this, it
was likely ignored at first because it simply didn't fit
the mold that was built by the research goal
expectations.

Admittedly, there was a wee bit of confirmation
bias [29] going on in these efforts that had not gone
unnoticed or compensated for initially; a condition
that is all but unavoidable in such ventures. However,
knowing full well that this was going on in the
background at certain points, balancing efforts were
still, in fact, continually underway to favor anything
that disputed findings and conclusions.

This purposeful finger on the unbalanced scale was quite fortunate. When the time was right, throwing this obsolete definition into the research mix rocked the project to its core in one way and shed light upon Ritual's writers in another way. The resulting insights brought a delight-filled smile to this researcher's countenance.

This was not unexpected either. Like so many Rituals spread throughout the world, such as the Preston-Webb style Rituals used by the majority of the jurisdictions operating within the United States of America, each of them hints at the use of a plethora of obsolete definitions required to comprehend the masked meanings of their passages.

As with many deliberate encrypting schemes, the use of obsolete definitions within secret[30] and peculiar[31] communication is a perfect way to hide meaning from those ill- or uninformed. Writers know this method hides meaning in plain sight. It banks upon the reality that the uninformed masses almost always assume currently used meanings, and rarely if ever consider the odd, unusual or archaic, much less obsolete. This is not because they overlook them. It's because they simply are unaware they exist or, through force of habit, dismiss them as irrelevant or no longer applicable. None but the well-informed see through these masks and into the core of what is offered.

This is the situation that the word *perfect* offers to you through Masonic ritual. Its writers knew that only a select few going through the ceremonies that use them had the background to understand what is offered by them. The majority experiencing them for the first time had yet to be *informed* and the writers even state and imply this within the ritual several times.

Ritual examples abound! Listed below are but a few of the typical terms within publicly available outdated and unused Blue Lodge Rituals where this issue is clearly conveyed.

1. *"...<u>inform</u> the Tyler ..."*
2. *"...*inform *[the Candidate]..."*
3. *"...the Worshipful Master is <u>informed</u> ..."*
4. *"...it becomes my duty to* inform *you [the Candidate] ..."*
5. *"...as you [the Candidate] are yet <u>uninformed</u>, ..."*
6. *"...your [<u>well-informed</u>] Conductor will answer for you..."*
7. *"...the Worshipful Master should be <u>informed</u>..."*
8. *"[the Candidate was]...<u>informed</u> that ..."*
9. *"...he <u>informed</u> me [the Candidate] ..."*
10. *"...were you [the Candidate] then <u>informed</u>?..."*
11. *"...<u>inform</u> the Worshipful Master..."*
12. *"...you <u>informed</u> me [the Candidate] ..."*
13. *"... you [the Candidate] are to converse with <u>well-informed</u> Brethren, who will be always as ready to give as you will be ready to receive instruction."*
14. *"In the character of a Master Mason, you [the now <u>informed</u> Brother] are authorized to correct the errors and irregularities of your <u>uninformed</u> brethren, and to guard them against a breach of fidelity.*
15. *"Universal benevolence you [the now <u>informed</u> Brother] are always to cultivate; and, by the regularity of your own behavior, afford the best example for the conduct of others <u>less informed</u>."*

These degrees convey clearly three accepted points about being informed:

1. Candidates are treated initially *as uninformed;*
2. The Brethren *are* believed *to be informed;*
3. Candidates *are to be informed* by the Brethren *through Ritual instruction.*

This issue of being informed is further emphasized by writers and lecturers within the first two centuries since the Premier Grand Lodge formed in London. One such writer, Brother Oliver, has several passages written within his book, *The Freemason's Treasury,* pointing out this very issue. His thoughts are shown below with the sections alluding to being *ill-informed* or *well-informed* in **bold** type.

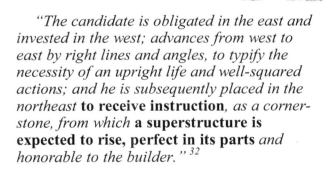

Here's a passage denoting the lodge's duty to instruct the Candidate…

"The candidate is obligated in the east and invested in the west; advances from west to east by right lines and angles, to typify the necessity of an upright life and well-squared actions; and he is subsequently placed in the northeast **to receive instruction***, as a cornerstone, from which* **a superstructure is expected to rise, perfect in its parts** *and honorable to the builder."* [32]

And here the Worshipful Master's duties to himself, to the Lodge and to the Candidates:

"A W. Master, indeed, may, by the mere force of memory, unaccompanied by either genius or talent, conduct the proceedings of a Lodge respectably for a time, and excite sentiments of admiration in a superficial observer; but he is still only a machine, the mainspring being his book of reference. Take away that, and in a few months his memory will fail him, and his popularity will ooze gradually away as detached portions of his lesson evaporate from his recollection. I have known individual Masons who could repeat the whole of the three lectures by rote from one end to the other, and yet were entirely ignorant of Masonry. **Instead of burdening the memory with a medley of words before they are correctly understood, the Masonic student would be better employed in learning to arrange and classify his ideas by systematic study and calm reflection; otherwise he will never merit the character of a bright and perfect Mason.**

"But, unfortunately, in many of our Lodges words are substituted for thought, and sometimes for knowledge itself. *Ask some of our W. Masters for the explanation of a particular sign, symbol, or doctrine, and he will answer in the unchanged language of the Ritual; but if a new inquiry be framed, even out of his own reply, he will be sensible of his deficiency; and, being at a loss for a solution of the difficulty, will probably say that the question is not in the Lecture Book.* **But if the W. Master study the forms and ceremonies attentively, and make himself acquainted with the reasons for every minute rite and**

every new situation, he need not fear but words will flow freely and without impediment to express his meaning.

"**The effects of initiation on a candidate depend, in a great measure, on the tact and knowledge of the Master**; *and the York Constitutions direct that he shall take especial care, in the admission of an Apprentice, that he do his Lord no prejudice; that he shall harbour no thief or thief's retainer, lest the Graft should come to shame; and if he unknowingly admit an improper person, he shall discharge him from the work when his inability is discovered.*

"*These are paramount and indispensable duties, and he is bound to perform them punctually and impartially. And in the reception of his Apprentice, if the preliminary ceremony be well conducted,* **it cannot fail to produce an impression which will prevent all misconception on the nature and object of the system**, *and silence any rising doubt which might have a tendency towards its disparagement. And further,* **the W. Master is strictly bound by another ancient Landmark to instruct his Apprentice faithfully** by "**teaching him all the various secrets of his Craft, and make him a perfect workman.**" *[33]*

Finally, here's yet another passage once more indicating the importance of the Candidate being well-informed, especially by his well-informed Brethren as his guardians.

"*The two latter members of our triad are*

denominated by our continental Brethren Pierre Brute and Pierre Cubique. The former is an imperfect unhewn stone, rough as when taken out of the quarry, but, being subjected to the skill and industry of the workman, **it is soon brought into due form** *and rendered fit for its place in the intended building. What can be a more appropriate emblem of the mind of man in its infant and primitive state, rough and unpolished like that unformed stone torn from its native rock and presented to the eye in no definite shape? It is, indeed, an apt type of mental ignorance and childish imbecility.* **But, under the influence of education, and by a judicious system of training, scintillations of genius begin to appear; and, being aided by the pious**

example of parents or guardians, the intellectual powers are called into action; reason, penetration, perception, and judgment become cultivated, and the ripened man is at length rendered a polished member of civilized society.

"In Masonic language, he becomes a Perfect Ashlar, or cubical polished stone, *which is so exactly true in all its dimensions as to be incapable of any test but that of the square and compasses, as an undeniable proof of perfect symmetry.* **It thus symbolizes the matured individual passing a blameless life in the uniform practice of piety and**

devotion; with a mind squared and polished by the influence of religion and virtue, till its moral integrity can only be tried and tested by the unerring standard of God's Word and an approving conscience." [34]

You might at this moment be asking yourself why I have been harping so much upon the issue of being *well-informed* and how this relates to this entire document's focus – *perfect.* And you would be right in asking this. Had I not stumbled upon the aforementioned obsolete definition, I too would be scratching my head and asking the same thing at this moment.

Not So Obsolete

That obsolete definition that I stumbled upon is the key to all this confusion for this current chapter, this book and for the Craft as well! In the definition's footnote, there was a reference to Shakespeare and how he used the word *perfect* within his many writings. There within was also an example provided:

*"I am **perfect** that the Pannonians and Dalmatians for their liberties are now in arms; a precedent which not to read would show the Britons cold: So Cæsar shall not find them."* [35]

At first glance, the passage confused me. It didn't read smoothly when I substituted all the current definitions usually applied to the word *perfect.* However, once I substituted the obsolete definitions, it began to make perfect sense. One by one I substituted the obsolete definitions and the passage came to life for me.

- *I am* **well-informed** *that the Pannonians and Dalmatians for their liberties are now in arms; a precedent which not to read would show the Britons cold: So Cæsar shall not find them.*

- *I am* **certain** *that the Pannonians and Dalmatians for their liberties are now in arms; a precedent which not to read would show the Britons cold: So Cæsar shall not find them.*

- *I am* **sure** *that the Pannonians and Dalmatians for their liberties are now in arms; a precedent which not to read would show the Britons cold: So Cæsar shall not find them.*

At that moment I became both excited and curious as to how many other examples could be found within Shakespeare's writings that would also have this obsolete definition apply successfully.

I went to an on-line compendium and searched the entirety of its records of his offered works. I found two hundred some odd variations of the word *perfect* within its reach. Of these occurrences, there were fifty-five examples where only the word *perfect* occurred rather than variations such as *imperfect, perfection, perfectly,* and others. As I went through reading each of these fifty-five passages containing the word *perfect* it became extremely clear that the obsolete definition was used by Shakespeare in far too many cases to be ignored as suspect.

In passage after passage the obsolete definitions were applied and the passages came alive with meaning hidden from the imperfect mind. I was amazed at how much was lost to me by not knowing Shakespeare's intended meaning. I realized only now that I was imperfect as to how his meaning was intended.

Revamping

I went to work immediately creating a quick reference dictionary for myself so I would not lose what I had uncovered. The words were written out at first...

- **Perfect, imperfect, perfectly, imperfectly, perfection,** and **imperfection**

I then applied the obsolete definitions that came forth through Shakespeare's use...

- **Perfect** – Well-informed; sure; certain
- **Imperfect** – Uninformed; unsure; uncertain
- **Perfectly** – Surely; certainly
- **Imperfectly** – Unsurely; uncertainly
- **Perfection** – Well-informedness; sureness; certainty
- **Imperfection** – Uninformedness, unsureness; uncertainty

As I completed the list and suitable definitions, as applied within Shakespeare's work, I sat in silent contemplation. There was an unsettlingly but recognizable pattern in his use. He was not applying any definitions used today.

Shakespeare's use of the word *perfect* left questions within my mind. Could it be that the introduction of the word *perfect* into our Rituals was an intentional breadcrumb trail, *a nineteenth-century version of a hyperlink,* to this obsolete definition? And even though the time-frame of application was off (the word initially applied to one of the lodge's jewels in the early part of the nineteenth century), were the innovators of our Craft Ritual at that time intending to draw attention to these obsolete definitions so that those looking past the superficial definitions would be rewarded for their efforts? Could it be that the innovations were making every effort to send a message to those who sought perfect Light?

Four and one-half centuries after Shakespeare's time, Brother Oliver's use of the word *perfect* in his above-quoted passages clearly indicated that *education* and *instruction* were always involved in bringing about the *perfect mason, perfect workman* and *perfect ashlar* (which itself symbolized the former two). Within context, the meaning of the word is evident. The obsolete meaning is more suitable to its use within these quotes than any other definition that could be considered.

How much more investigation should be done to confirm that the *perfect ashlar* is not one that is flawless but rather one that is well-informed and suitable to specific ends?

I was compelled to investigate further.

Reassessing

I went back to Ritual and began to look at the word *perfect* in a different Light. I combed through each passage with fresh eyes. Passage after passage confirmed my thoughts. One such passage within an offered catechism, also known as *proficiency*, reads as follows:

Q. What are the movable jewels?

A. The rough ashler, the perfect ashler, and the trestle-board.

Q. What are they?

A. Rough ashler is a stone in its rough and natural state; the perfect ashler is also a stone, made ready by the working-tools of the fellow craft, to be adjusted in the building; and the trestle-board is for the master workman to draw his plans and designs upon.

Q. Of what do they remind us?

A. By the rough ashler **we are reminded** of our rude and imperfect state by nature; **by the perfect ashler of that state of perfection at which we hope to arrive by a virtuous education, our own endeavors, and the blessing of God;** and by the trestle-board we are also reminded that, as the operative workman erects his temporal building agreeably to the rules and designs laid down by the Master on his trestle-board, so should we, both operative and speculative, endeavor to erect our spiritual building agreeably to the rules and designs laid down by the Supreme Architect of the universe, in the great book of Revelation, which is our spiritual, moral, and Masonic trestle-board.

The passages referring to the perfect ashlar stood out in a way that they had not done so before this moment. They were not pointing toward being flawless at all. Clearly, the *perfection* that ritual pointed toward was a direct result of education – once again putting forth the need for being *well-informed, sure* and *certain!*

VI. Perfect Assumptions

"There are more things in heaven and earth, Horatio,
Than are dreamt of in your philosophy."
– Hamlet; William Shakespeare

As research progressed, I paused and asked myself if there would be any confusion presented in the minds of Light seekers had I just left the term *well-informed* dangling. There was a high risk that some well-meaning Brother would take this term and try to understand it out of context or worse, explain it to another Brother using another ill-defined word or term as a substitute, which occurs more often than not.

This was a scary thought and highly probable. So much of membership actions when it comes to what is thought of as education is merely stuffing knowledge between one's ears and providing it on the spot when the right buttons are pressed to warrant retrieving and sharing it.

Would there be any difference between being *well-informed* and being what was considered *knowledgeable* in these situations? I wanted to immediately say, *"not really"* and rightfully so. Using the term to indicate huge amounts of retrievable inventory does no justice to what well-informed was ever intended to convey. Or does it?

If you were to do a quick look up on either term you might get the impression that they were synonymous.

> **Knowledgeable** – *intelligent, educated and well-informed*

> **Well-Informed** – *having or showing much knowledge about a wide range of subjects, or about one particular subject*

We could leave it there if we were so inclined to take the first things offered. We could take the two terms to mean the same thing and use them interchangeably from that moment on, and who would be none-the-wiser?

However, things are not always the same underneath the surface and in this case it is an understatement. To be responsible to our research, we must once again delve into context and apply what we find to what is offered within ritual.

Knowledgeable

When we examine the word *knowledgeable*, we find that it didn't always mean what it's taken to mean today. The etymology of the word shows this:

> **Knowledgeable** *(adj.)also knowledgable, c. 1600, "capable of being known, recognizable" (a 17c. sense now obsolete), from knowledge in its Middle English verbal sense + -able. The sense of "having knowledge, displaying mental capacity" is from 1829 and probably a new formation[36].*

At the time that ritual was first being standardized, the word had to do with capability. It was not until later on that it had to do with the resource, the experience, and the skill backing these.

Then there are the assumptions of intelligence. So often it's taken for granted that people with a lot of information are knowledgeable and therefore intelligent. It's not until you talk with such people at any length that you begin to see whether they know what they are talking about or simply spouting out information in line with what they have been instructed to spew. If they have any depth of worthwhile knowledge, they are capable of using their information prudently and in line with what is properly required of this information based upon suitable experience.

Well-Informed

When we examine the term *well-informed*, we may also make certain assumptions that would appear to be proper within the context of superficial assessment. We might take that a well-informed individual was intelligent because they appear to have sufficient information at their immediate disposal to converse on a topic without looking ignorant. As before, who would be none-the-wiser for assuming so?

Examining the term's definitions, recent and obsolete, we get an entirely different feel for it. Focusing upon those definitions that apply to ritual, and keeping in mind that the term is implied through the use of the word *perfect*, we get a sense as to what was intended.

Ritual continually alludes to *well-informed* having to do with *education*. This is not just any type of education. It is a specific regimen that *shapes & refines* those who undergo this *great & important undertaking* so that they are transformed within and without. That transformation is symbolized by the transition from a *rough* ashlar to a *smooth* or *perfect* ashlar.

And this is where an obsolete definition for the term comes into play that perfectly describes this. In 1590, Edmund Spenser's, The Faerie Queene, III.vi:

"... after Nilus invndation, / Infinite shapes of creatures men do fynd, / Informed in the mud, on which the Sunne hath shynd..."

The now-obsolete meaning of the word *informed* used within his play was *created; given form.* When we examine what Candidates undergo through the education in which they should engage, the end-in-mind is to create and give form to them as symbolized by the *perfect* a.k.a. *well-informed* ashlar.

All this transformation occurs as a direct result and consequence of the specific education and the Work supposedly provided by the Lodge of Brothers in whom the Candidates place their trust.

However, when the provided education is focused strictly upon making men functioning members of the lodge rather than making good men better, the only thing that is transformed are Candidates into members. When this is all that occurs, both the Lodge and the newly formed members miss out on the change intended by what Ritual points members toward – *A Deliberate Transformation though the Betterment of Good Men!*

VII. Perfect Points

It was only after putting to rest the question of obsolete definitions and how they apply to the *perfect ashlar* that an impulse arose to revisit an unresolved issue of the past. The issue was written about in my previous works and it was never put to rest with any great satisfaction. That issue was why the

Points of Entrance were referred to as *Perfect*.

From any outward indication, the modern definition of the word *perfect* required a lot of justification when anyone tried to explain these points and why they were deemed *perfect*. Adding to this forced and very awkward defining were the obvious changes in Rituals that have occurred over the years which changed these perfect points from three points to four in some jurisdictions.

Additionally, the recently applied obsolete *well-informed* meaning simply didn't fit, even when forced!

Not to be deterred from facing the issue head-on, one of the sets was addressed first.

Three Points

When researching the Perfect Points many years ago, there were several versions presented to me. One version had only three Perfect Points and it was presented in a Prestonian catechism.[37] An excerpt from a publicly known but retired and unused ritual goes like this:

Q. How do you know yourself to be a Mason?
A. By having been examined and approved, well reported of, and regularly initiated into the Order.

Q. How will you convince me that you are a Mason?
A. By signs, tokens, and *perfect points of entrance.*

Q. What are signs?
A. All squares, angles, levels and perpendiculars are good and sufficient signs to know Masons by.

Q. What purpose do they serve?
A. To distinguish a Mason in the light

Q. What are tokens?
A. Certain friendly and brotherly words and grips, which distinguish a Mason in the dark as well as in the light.

Q. Will you give me the [perfect] *points of entrance?*
A. Give me the first and I will give you the second.

Q. I hele.
A. I conceal...

Q. What do you conceal?
A. All secrets and mysteries belonging to Free Masons in Masonry, except it be to a true and lawful Brother for his caution.

Q. But as I am the examiner, *you may safely reveal to me the points of entrance...*
A. Of,[38] at, and on.

Q. Of, at, and on what?
A. *Of my own free-will and accord, at the door of the Lodge, and on the point of a sharp implement.*

The first point addresses the Candidate's volition. It clarifies the need for the Candidate to enter freely and without duress. It spotlights the exercise of his free-will in his joining the fraternity.

The second point addresses the need for the Candidate to move from the profane world to the world of the temple. It alludes to crossing a threshold, a bourne, from which there is no return.

The third point addresses the importance of keeping what is to be shared as confidential and the consequence of breaking one's word.

What makes these Points of Entrance *Perfect*? It's not an easy correlation. Upon reviewing some of the previously disclosed[39] and applicable meanings assigned to the word *perfect*, the ones that stand out *perfectly* and within reason are 1) satisfying all requirements, 2) corresponding to an ideal standard or abstract concept, 3) legally valid, and 4) complete.

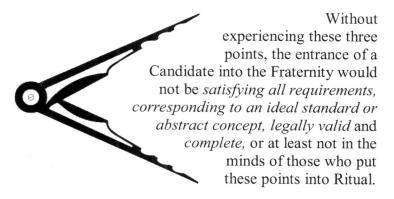

Without experiencing these three points, the entrance of a Candidate into the Fraternity would not be *satisfying all requirements, corresponding to an ideal standard or abstract concept, legally valid* and *complete,* or at least not in the minds of those who put these points into Ritual.

Four Points

A different version of these *Perfect Points* is found within the dominant Preston-Webb style rituals used commonly within the United States of America. A passage from publicly available but retired and unused rituals goes something like this:

Q: ...I now require you to explain to me the [perfect] points of your entrance: how many, and what are they?

A. They are four: the Guttural, the Pectoral, the Manual, and the Pedestal, which allude to the four cardinal virtues...

This version is usually tied directly to the four cardinal virtues. That being said, it is difficult to assign any meaning to these four locations on the body and it requires some consideration and review of what is actually going on during the ceremony.

Let's point out some of these meanings.

The **Guttural** refers to the throat. It is with this that a Candidate puts forth their desire to join the

Fraternity. This also addresses the *free-will* aspects alluded to in the set of three perfect points discussed previously. The Guttural is also what he uses to affirm his belief in God. It is with this that he obligates himself. It is with this reference that he recognizes and acknowledges what he loses when he is not being true to his word.

The **Pectoral** refers to the chest. This is where a Candidate's heart is housed, the very place where he is first prepared to become a Mason within the Fraternity. This is where he is reminded sharply of the instruction that is to follow and the consequences of misuse of that instruction. This also addresses the "sharp implement" aspects alluded to in the set of three perfect points discussed previously. This is where he holds in confidence that which is sacredly shared by others and where he holds the instructions that are deposited. It is with this reference that he recognizes and acknowledges what he loses when he is not being true to his word.

The **Manual** refers to the hands. It is with these that a Candidate signs his petitions. It is with these that he takes upon himself his solemn and binding obligations. It is with these that he first takes the hand of a Brother to welcome him into the Fraternity and to learn how to recognize Brothers in light and darkness. It is with this reference that he recognizes and acknowledges what he loses when he is not being true to his word.

The **Pedestal**, also known as "The Pedal", refers to the feet. It is with these that a Candidate enters into the lodge. This also addresses the "entering into the lodge" aspects alluded to in the set of three perfect points discussed previously. It is with these that he

moves about the lodge. It is with these that he first
approaches the Altar towards becoming a Brother. It
is with this reference that he recognizes and
acknowledges what he loses when he is not being true
to his word.

What makes these four *Perfect* Points of Entrance
better than, or an improvement upon, the previously
discussed three? It appears to be a much easier
correlation to what occurs for the Candidate within
Rituals. These four allude to many more aspects of
entrance than do the previously discussed three.

Upon reviewing some of the earlier disclosed[40]
and applicable meanings assigned to the word *perfect*,
the definitions that stand out *perfectly* and within
reason are similar to the three Perfect Points before.
They are 1) satisfying all requirements,
2) corresponding to an ideal standard or abstract
concept, 3) legally valid, and 4) complete.

As with the three points, without experiencing
these four points, the entrance of anyone into the
Fraternity would not be *satisfying all requirements,
corresponding to an ideal standard or abstract
concept, legally valid* and *complete,* or at least, once
again, in the minds of those who put these points into
the ritual. Having all these meanings satisfied during
the ceremony points to an entrance that was *perfect.*

Five Points

In researching the perfect points, there was disclosed yet another set of perfect points by an article appearing in Pietre-Stones called *The Perfect Points of Entrance.* It was by Bro. Prof. Dr. U. Gauthamadas, a member of Lodge Prudentia No.369 of the Grand Lodge of India. What follows is a small representation of disclosed points for future considerations.

Q: How were you made a freemason?
A: By the perfect points of my entrance.

Q: What were the perfect points of your entrance?
A: Preparation, obligation, sign, grip or token and word.

It's not clear as to the validity of what is written of within his article.

However, the validity of its insights offered echoes the same aspects of *perfect* discussed earlier. As stated before, without experiencing what these points allude to, the entrance of a Candidate into the Fraternity would not be *satisfying all requirements, corresponding to an ideal standard or abstract concept, legally valid* and *complete,* or at least in the minds of those who put these points into Ritual.

Once again, this is the purpose of the Perfect Points. Each Jurisdiction has its own way of ensuring that its Candidates experience specific things to guarantee they are brought into their organizations *perfectly* and without exception.

VIII. Perfect Lodges et Alia

Further research revealed yet another *perfect* related passage that showed up within a variety of different rituals. The phrase using the term is put forth after a Candidate is asked what makes a perfect lodge. The response to the question usually includes something like the following:

> *"...three form a Lodge, and five may hold it, seven only can make it perfect..."*

As can be expected, there are a variety of different reasons provided within different rituals as to why seven is the number required. The numbers of members usually dominate the explanation landscape.

However, not one reason points in the direction that is most obvious. This is understandable since the majority of members are not *well-informed* as to rhetorical thinking – a necessary training that brings about symbolic awareness and understanding.

In this instance, the number seven is used not as an indicator of quantity. It is not to be taken literally. It is used to symbolize quality. That quality is one of *completeness.* This use of the number seven stems back to ancient times and comes from the counting of days between the four primary moon phases; that number being seven. With each change in the phase of the moon, another seven days have passed and reflect a completed phase has occurred and the start of another. Since ancient times the use of the number seven has indicated this completeness.

There are numerous other examples as well. As this number is applied to a *perfect lodge,* the use within ritual is the same; it is indicating that the lodge is *complete.*

Brother Mackey alluded to this when he wrote about it within his Encyclopedia. Under the heading of a *Just Lodge* he has the following:

> *"A Lodge is said to be Just, Perfect, and Regular under the following circumstances:*
> *Just, when it is furnished with the three Great Lights; Perfect, when it contains the constitutional number of members; and Regular, when it is working under a Charter of Warrant of Constitution emanating from the legal authority."*

Once again, this is where rhetorical training comes into play and it is crucial to understanding the symbolic nature of what is conveyed. This training tells us that literal meaning must be transcended and metaphors must be embraced and applied for intended meaning to be grasped. In this case, this training tells us that numbers are not to be taken quantitatively; they are to be taken qualitatively!

Another example of this is the number *forty*. It must not be taken quantitatively but qualitatively when used within symbolic conveyances. When used in this manner, it indicates *"trials; testing"*. The use of this within scripture occurs numerous times, such as indicated by the years in the desert Moses wandered, the days in the wilderness Jesus fasted and the days and nights of rain Noah experienced.

And just like the number forty is used symbolically, the number seven is not to be taken as a quantity, but as a quality when conveying symbolic insights.

As stated before, the number seven indicates *completeness.* As this number is applied to lodges, a complete or *perfect* lodge has present the constitutional required number of members. The quantity depends upon the jurisdiction. However, the quality is represented symbolically by the number seven, regardless of the quantity called out for.

Reviewing the definitions assigned to the word *perfect* we quickly find that that it has a meaning aligned with all that has been put forth herein – *complete.* Repairing to the phrase that sent us down this rabbit hole and substituting the word *complete* for the word *perfect* we get the following:

> *"...three form a Lodge, and five may hold it, seven only can make it <u>complete</u>..."*

This is exactly what Brother Mackey was saying when he wrote:

"...Perfect, when it contains the constitutional number of members; ..."

The Perfect Master

There are further studies and research that you can engage in far beyond the Blue Lodge system should you want to pursue further light on this topic. One such direction is exploring other occurrences of the word *perfect* within rituals around the globe. I recommend you direct your attention first to the titles found within the Scottish Rite Degrees. There are two degrees specifically that have the word *perfect* within the title, except within the Northern Jurisdiction of the USA (where just the 5th degree has the word *Perfect* in the title). Those degrees are:

- The 5th Degree - *Perfect Master*
- The 14th Degree - *Perfect Elu, Grand Elect Perfect and Sublime Mason*, or *Grand Elect Perfect and Sublime Master* (depending upon which jurisdiction you explore)

You might want to start your research by experiencing the degrees for yourself. Once experienced, there are many directions you can take your research from there.

As for me, this researcher has come to his own conclusions as to what the word *perfect* means when applied to these titles. What are *your* thoughts?

IX. Operative to Speculative

*Metaphors and allegories are verbal or visual
vehicles designed to deliver underlying truths
about ourselves and what we deal with. When
you take such vehicles as factual rather than
the truths they are intended to convey, you lose
all insight into what they were intended to
communicate and use them to pursue things
that never existed.*

As my
research
continued, I did a
reality check. So
much of the
speculative
process is filled
with lofty
statements with
very few of them actually being pursued as an actual
instruction set acted out by Candidates.

I wanted to know how close the speculative
process followed the operative process. What was the
process that Stonecrafters used to pull stones from the
ground, judge, move, shape, raise and finally position
and cement them into place within a structure? How
did the speculative process differ in principle from the
operative process and why did the differences exist?

What would I find if I opened myself up to
inspection? I endeavored in my pursuit of answers.

The research was disturbingly revealing. The
speculative process is so simplified within
Freemasonic ritual that it's nearly unrecognizable as

anything that would come close to operative, even when speculation is taken into consideration. As many members find, who have done similar examinations, exceedingly little of the *speculative* process of bringing new members into and up through the Craft resembles the operative.

In previous writings, I traced ashlar development through an Operative's eyes and juxtaposed it within a Speculative's experience. In the paper, the whole journey from quarry to building was examined and put to print. That paper eventually was turned into a catechism and immortalized within the book, *Building Hiram.* The Craft development process was also examined in detail within *The Craft Unmasked.*

I've learned even more since those efforts.

Due to this current writing's focus, it is necessary to review this process a bit and include some of the findings of that effort and subsequent research. I shall repeat them briefly herein and share suitable information that supports these writing's directions.

The Quarry

Rocks are cut from the earth to create three primary materials. The first material is cubic stone. The second is façade stone. The last is fill stone.

All three have their purposes. The first stone is used to create structure. The second is used to augment appearance. The third is used to create sounder structures.

Cubic Stones are any three dimensional stone whose measurements are greater than two inches in any one direction. They are typically freestones that are chosen, and their choice is dependent upon their intended use. The character of each stone was such that none of its perceived flaws would prevent it from being utilized for the builder's use, whether it was freestone or not. In other words, each chosen stone was most likely flawed in some way but still usable.

The use of the cubic stone was for structural purposes. They were used to create the structure of what was to be built. Under no circumstances was a cubic stone to be used that could not stand up to the load-bearing needs of the structure intended. To do so was to risk the integrity of the building and the safety of those involved in its use.

I shall leave it to the imagination of the reader to apply these metaphorical characteristics to what they see at play within the Freemasonic organization.

Façade Stones, also known as *bastard ashlars*, were used to cover the structural stones. They were shaped and textured to provide for the appearance of the building as a whole. They were also used to cover up structural stone flaws whose primary function was for support and not for appearance.

Although these stones had dimension, there was at least one of their dimensions that was so shallow, that the stone could not stand the stresses involved in load-bearing. Hence their use as covering and show, leaving the load-bearing task for those stones which could.

As before, I shall leave it to the imagination of the reader to apply this metaphorically to what they see within the organization of Free & Accepted Masons.

Fill Stones were just that. They were used as fill between inner and outer walls and other areas where voids and hollows required additional support, but not appearance. Their task was to provide for a more solid structure, especially where failure would occur if those spaces were not filled with stone solid enough to support and brace the surrounding stones.

Once again, I shall leave it to the imagination of the reader to apply this metaphorically to what they see within the Freemasonic Order.

Although all types are crucial to building, it is the former two types that come into play.

The Site

Whether the work on these two aforementioned stones is at the quarry or onsite is not up for debate. The fact is these stones need to be worked to bring them from their crude state (rough) to their  usable state (perfected). They are called *rough ashlars* at this stage and remain thus labeled until they are worked upon.

The moment said stones are worked upon is the moment they are then called *common ashlars.* It's typically the apprentices doing this work, and doing so under the supervision and guidance of well-informed workers.

Once stones are perfected, that is, at the point where they are cut to form and ready for raising, positioning and cementing, they are referred to as *Perfect Ashlars*. No ashlar is raised, positioned or cemented into place until it is perfected, that is, suitable for the builder's use.

Speculative Practice

When we take this process and apply it symbolically to what we do as Freemasons, we get a far different picture than what we are usually told. If you were to query members of the Craft, you would find that many of them are likely to tell you that perfection is impossible even though the process of perfecting is clearly put before them within the speculative model of advancement. It is often not seen though because very few members take the time to think through the process. Instead, they simply default to what they are told.

Let's go through this now.

A person who is not a member is called a *profane.* A profane is viewed as a *rough ashlar* by the Craft. Should a profane decide to petition for membership, an examination team would go through a process to determine if he is a good man, of sound mind, good rapport, and well-recommended, along with other qualifiers. He may be voted upon for membership after the interview committee provides a favorable report. If accepted as a Candidate, he would enter through the west gate as a rough ashlar to receive his First Degree. Once he receives this Degree, he is still a rough ashlar for he has yet to start his Work.

Much like in operative masonry, once an Apprentice starts his Work, his ashlar is called a *common ashlar.* You will likely never hear this term used within the Freemasonic Order though. Freemasonry does not go into the detail one might expect it to in such matters. It's not until his Apprentice Work is completed and readied for *raising* that it is called *a perfect ashlar.* This understanding too is not commonly acknowledged within the Craft.

Freemasonic work is called *proficiencies,* even though such proficiencies truly demand nothing more than memorizing and returning scripted words and choreography. Once this activity is completed a Candidate is permitted to advance.

Advancing to the Fellow Craft level, he is once again asked to repeat another proficiency at this level, with the same outcome.

Once completed, he is then advanced to the third level of the Blue Lodge where he is asked to do more of the same.

Reexamination

If all this seems shallow and nothing like the process Stonecraft masons would use, you would be right in your observation. There is far more involved in Speculative Craft Masonry than what is usually asked of by those who advance you for organizational purposes. But should you desire to get more from your investment, you will need to go beyond what is commonly expected by your Brothers.

Let's go back to the Work of the Apprentice; not the proficiencies, but the actual Work that the Apprentice Degree points Candidates to do in order to move them from one stage to another. This transformational process takes place by doing the Work pointed toward by the degree. It is through this Work that he transforms, as in *perfects* himself and readies himself for the challenges of the next stage. His Work would have brought order to the chaos of his heart, a task that is only done as one transforms.

Once he completes this Work he is now the perfected ashlar. That Candidate, who has prepared himself, goes about raising himself by climbing the last seven steps pointed toward by the Staircase Lecture. Should he take upon himself the next grand and important undertaking, he would thoroughly study the seven liberal arts and sciences. His efforts would bring order to the chaos of his mind for he would have raised himself through successfully undertaking and completing this stage of his Work.

At that point, he would be readied to be positioned and cemented into *that house not made with hands* that is the Fraternity. Too often, this is viewed as the whole point of the Third Degree. In reality, it is receiving either *a title* for doing the minimum work of proficiencies or *an acknowledgment* for Work previously done by those who have done it fully.

You'll see that the challenge each member of the Craft faces is understanding the difference between the advancement work required by one's membership and the advancement Work required by one as a human being.

The former activity focuses only upon whether you can act well as a member. The latter activity focuses upon whether you can perfect yourself as a human being and apply this successfully toward all life activities.

This process has never been about ongoing and never-ending improvement. It's about specific milestones and achievements – *stages!*

This means arriving at various points of development where you're no longer what you once were. By doing the Work and doing so in stages, you are much more than you were in the previous stages and all for the better!

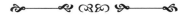

X. The Key Stone

Sometimes keys to doors you seek to open are found in places you least expect to find them and look nothing like what you had imagined.

It was clear from what was known about operative practices that the perfect ashlar used within 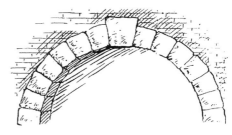 speculative practice denoted stones made ready for use by the workmen. Each was perfected toward suitability. No such stone would ever be raised before it was made ready.

This made sense. The premature raising of any stone was to be avoided at all costs since this took away from what the workforce should be worked upon. To progress stones prematurely would unduly burden those who would raise, position and cement it into place. Premature stones were unsuitable for what was to come because they required additional Work to make them fit in. Their progress was halted to ensure that no one person involved in the process would have to do unnecessary Work.

In Plain Sight

Even Freemasonic rituals point to this important aspect of the Stonecraft process. The key is there for all to see. It was relatively early on in my research that I came across this key. It points to what the perfect ashlar actually denotes. We've all seen it, staring at us when we first walked into the Lodge room. It was pointed out also by the lectures that abundantly graced the ears and eyes of those going through the process as well. And it was one of those *hidden in plain sight* moments where I shook my head in embarrassment when I made the connection for the first time. I knew it made sense too.

Freemasons, and non-members alike, who look to the East see this key (although they may not recognize it as such). It's further stressed by your Brothers at least once as you progress, and thereafter every time you sit in on a lecture where this is pointed out.

What is this key?

It is what the first and second steps leading up to the East direct our attention toward.

The First Step

As it is described, this first step denotes several things. The first is the lowest elected officer who sits in the South. Additionally, it denotes the Apprentice, the lowest of all degrees. But part of the key that pulls it all together is what it also denotes – *Youth!*

This last implication is part of the key to what the Perfect Ashlar represents. The Apprentice is considered a Rough Ashlar when first he enters the Fraternity. As stated previously, when he works upon himself, that ashlar is then known as a Common Ashlar, but not to members of the Fraternity. Unfortunately, this term is a Stonecraft term only.

Once his work is completed, he transforms himself from a Youth to an Adult. He is considered an adult and ready to do the Fellow Craft Work. This transformation is clearly denoted by the second step above the first leading to the East – Fellow Craft and *Manhood! The second part of the key!*

There is only one thing that must change within a male to transform him from a youth to a man. That is he must mature!

Circling back to the purpose of the book and definitions offered by several resources having to do with the meanings one can assign to the word *perfect*, one of them aligns perfectly well with the transition an Apprentice must undergo – *Mature!*

The stone that makes for the first step to the East is the rough ashlar. It denotes the immaturity that Candidates must overcome to get to the second step.

The stone that makes for the second step to the East is the *perfect* ashlar. *That second step denotes the maturity that an Apprentice must develop to become that ashlar.*

The Connecting Ashlar

That key stone is important to understand. What it points toward is the Work direction of serious Apprentices and the ultimate end each can expect to reach should they successfully engage in the Work. This key also helps create the connection, or bond, which ties the perfect ashlar to the Work that must be undertaken by all Candidates who truly want what is pointed toward by the Ritual.

What is to follow directly reflects this end – *the maturation, as in, the perfecting, of our Masonic Youth.*

XI. The Perfecting Work

Put your Support where you're Nurtured Best.

To some, Lodges are at best no more than temporary homes from which Brothers travel from one

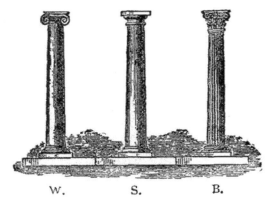

W.   S.   B.

working, earning, supporting and contributing situation to another. To make them anything other than these would be to bastardize their intent. To others, they are a way of being where Brothers drink deeply from the wellsprings of the spirit; making it a community of brothers, transformation and rejuvenation where all are paid their due wages for work well-performed.

Past Musings

I've heard it said by some Brothers and scholars that in days of old, Operative Lodges were convened for the purpose of performing work supported by financial sources other than the workers themselves. These Lodges came into being for that purpose and for that purpose alone. Once this work was completed, or became unsupported, as in, financial support stopped or dried up, the convened Lodge dissolved and the workmen traveled to find supported work elsewhere.

Perhaps it's a fantasy to think that these workmen operated with wisdom, where they only had a Lodge convened when supported work existed. Perhaps it was not wisdom at all and merely common sense that drove the practicality of such conventions. Either way, the *support* paradigm seemed to work very well at the time. Lodges came into being and left existence just as swiftly based upon some very simple practical drivers.

It made perfect sense to me that such paradigms might have dictated the creation and disbanding of such Operative Lodges. Both the Lodge and its workers required expenses to be paid on a regular basis. Lodges were business operations primarily and most business operations have overhead costs associated with running them. Working tools and materials must have been procured and maintained, at a cost. Administration and site support costs must also have been taken into account. These expenses and others must have been taken into consideration when work was to commence.

For such Lodges to come into and remain in existence, work supported by sources of revenue certainly needed to exist also. It's costly for workers of any lodge to exist in any moment when there are no supported works to be done. For workers to be supported in their efforts, fair compensation (revenue for their work) was required to sustain them. Once the support for such work ceased you could easily expect the entire workforce to disband and travel to other supported work sites known to the workers. I could see that it was a good business model as it still functions this way quite well in many parts of the world.

Present Musings

It's clear today that Speculative Lodges come into being not because there is externally supported work to be done. They come into being because there are groups of workers called *Brothers* who want to build and run lodges. The financial support no longer comes from external sources. It comes from the pockets of patrons consisting of member Brothers and degree Candidates. It no longer comes from financial backers or benefactors wanting structures built for one reason or another.

The work these lodges do has also changed. It's taken two different directions in its focus: the lodge (a band of Brothers who meet within a lodge room) and the individual workers (the Brothers themselves). In either case, work results cannot be seen as external edifices that tower over the heads of those who build them. Work results cannot be viewed as a bridge that leads to other destinations. The results of their Work are intangible in every respect and those desiring to

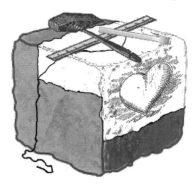

touch any of it shall die in frustration before they may lay finger upon it.

The work focus today is no longer Operative in nature. It is solely Speculative and internal, not just to the Lodge building but also to the lodge's patrons. These patrons profit from this Work and they are the workers themselves. The Work is explicit too. It's designed with one end in mind: to preserve a specific Code that, when applied, *Raises males to Maturity*.

Lodge Work

The work within the lodge building is totally *preservation-based*. It is esoteric in its nature but is often viewed and practiced as if it were exoteric. No matter how it may be viewed, preservation is always at the forefront of its purpose.

There is an established and honored work-flow. Future workers go through a rigorous interview process followed by work being Initiated. Should the new worker show commitment, he shall eventually Pass onto other work activities that eventually Raise him into providing the same support toward others so inclined.

Every stage of the process *preserves* the specific aforementioned Code, and only those who have committed that special Code to memory are allowed to work within the Lodge building and under the Lodge's work charter.

Worker Work

Many Lodge members don't clearly understand the Work that should take place within each of the workers. Even fewer support it. It's referred to as *esoteric* by some Brothers and *non-sense* by others. The end-in-mind of this Work is *Maturation* although, in the archaic language used by the workers, it is referred to as *Perfection*.

Strength Work

Workers who are new to the Work are referred to as *Apprentices*. The symbols used by the Craft to denote these workers all point toward Youth. These symbols also point toward the need for these youth to develop and use specific disciplines that allow for better self-management. Activities designed to unburden them of non-essential activities, relationships, ideas, and possessions are pointed out to these workers in the hope that they shall be mature enough to knowingly engage in them. There are also activities designed to strengthen their ability to make better choices and decisions. These too are offered to the workers in the hope that they shall be ready for them.

It's important to note that the Apprentice Work might appear to be focused upon the superficial aspects of the worker. There is much talk about making surfaces smooth and right, all symbolic allusions to internal Work. With well-guided instruction though, these aspects lift quickly away to reveal that it is not the external but internal character that is being Worked into being smooth and right. Their Work requires fervent and unwavering commitment.

Those workers without these qualities shall never pass suitably toward any worthwhile ends. It is these qualities that bring about the wages which each worker receives and in turn contributes to the Lodge as a unified workforce. Should they fall short in any way, they and their Brothers shall suffer together.

Wisdom Work

Workers who progress through the initial stages of the Work come to pass into a stage referred to as *Fellow Craft.* The symbols used by Craft to denote these workers all point toward Manhood. They

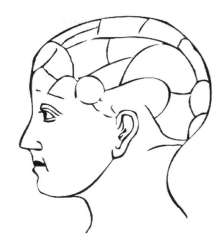

also point to the need for these men to develop and use specific disciplines that allow for mature management of things external to themselves. They are given an opportunity to engage in activities that show them how to distinguish things in progressively finer detail and to use both words and numbers as tools to do this. All these activities cultivate understandings within the workers that reveal order in a seemingly chaotic world. These activities also cultivate their understandings as to how seeming chaos can be ordered and controlled in very beneficial ways.

The Fellows' Work is bringing order to chaos, not to the external but internal worlds of workers – *their minds!* Hints to this Work are briefly mentioned in the Apprentice Degree but not focused upon at any length. However, it is explained in depth within the second Degree, and it is clearly a continuation of past foundation-building.

With well-guided instruction and a few examples, the Candidate, soon to be Craftsman, comes to understand that his internal world must be thoroughly Worked upon first. Only after this effort should he work upon his outside world. External work is tough, demanding and unforgiving. Those who are still burdened or who still lack strength shall find that they are incapable of rendering anything of satisfaction.

Furthermore, if they do not learn to distinguish well, their Work and what they earn as a result shall suffer greatly. It is the internal qualities of these workmen that shall bring about their eventual wages and in turn, what they shall contribute to the Lodge as a unified workforce. Should these workers be viewed superficially, all future benefits shall be diminished for all involved.

Beauty Work

Workers progressing well through Manhood raise their understandings and their discipline to rightfully merit the title of *Master.* They become shining examples of what recognizing, understanding and executing the preserved Code can do. Those who don't merit the title shall lessen the wages for the entire Lodge.

The symbols, used by the Craft to denote these workers, all point toward Age and Wisdom. They also denote the need for these men to further develop and use their well-honed understandings and disciplines in life. Workers who merit such a title also merit traveling, working, earning, supporting and contributing at the high level that they have achieved. Pretenders to this title may be given opportunity to do all five at first, but their lack of maturity, discipline, and skill shall soon betray them. Their very looks shall reveal to the world who they truly are.

Masters render beauty in their Work. Their lives reveal to others and the world that they have achieved Mastery and that allows for liberties not permitted by those less masterful. It is their qualities that bring about the wages they receive and, in turn, what they contribute to the Lodge as a unified workforce.

Lodge Work Revisited

Lodge members frustrated by the lack of sufficient support from poorly trained workers should contemplate long and hard upon the worker  Work that each Lodge should promote. Just as in the Operative workforces of years' past, Speculative workforces of present-day lodges require funding for lodge Work. Often times the Work itself provides the funding for lodge Work. This is because workers do not view lodge activities from a financial standpoint alone. Work in and of itself should and does have a high degree of satisfaction. It is always rendered as payment to those who joyfully engage in it.

When the Work being done no longer holds reward, the workforce shall disengage and leave. The Operative Lodges knew well that any work that goes unfunded is unrewarding. This especially applies to unrewarding Speculative Work.

When a lodge wants support, it is well advised to look at the Work that it provides to its Workers. A lodge engaged in activities that have no rewards to its workers shall continually struggle to keep workers in its quarry. An unpaid workforce will not remain out of loyalty; they will leave and go where they are rewarded best.

You might find yourself asking the question, *"What is that Work?"* Soon enough we will explore this at the Apprentice level.

Points to Perpend:

1) How does your Lodge nurture its members toward maturity as males?
2) What wages do your Lodge members currently receive for the Work that they do?
3) What wages would you like to see for your Work?
4) What Work must you commit to do and to perform to receive this desired Wage?
5) How soon should you be starting this Work?
6) Whom shall you ask to assist you toward your desired ends and how soon shall you ask them?

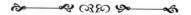

XII. Our Masonic Youth

*Are we expecting too much from
our youthful Brothers?*

Research
reflects what
our nation's
forefathers
knew long
ago: You
cannot expect
wisdom to be
a principle
component of

youthful activities. They believed this so strongly that
they incorporated this very ideal into our nation's
laws. Citizens must reach a specific age[41] before they
are considered eligible to hold important governing
positions. What did they know about maturity that we
should know as well?

There should be no doubt in any Masterful
Mason's mind that Masonic Work transforms men
toward the better. It does this by engaging their hearts
and minds in activities designed to Work areas of the
brain that promote improved and mature thinking.
These areas are specific and Masons who engage in
helping others develop should take note of these areas
early on to determine this Work's effectiveness.

One standard of effective measurement is
maturity. Masonic coaches and mentors should well
acquaint themselves with methods that can both
develop and ascertain maturity in those they are asked

to assist in Masonic Work. It might occur to those Brothers who have considered deeply the current state of the Craft that their failure to mature the Lodge weakens the Fraternity daily and causes Brothers to focus attention on superfluous matters and activities. Reviewing the division between Youth and Manhood might be a good starting point for those interested in being a force for change within the Craft.

Youth

It might surprise some people to know that adulthood does not begin between ages 18 and 21. Yes, this is considered the *legal* age of consent and the time when those who reach it can and do take on many *adult* activities and responsibilities. It is also around the time when a person is judged and held accountable as an adult. This age is also long past when participation in biological reproduction can and does occur.

The benchmarks set up by modern society as the transition point between Youth and Adulthood is not however when biological adulthood begins. Authentic adulthood in humans occurs several years later on, and in some cases, much later on, if at all.[42]

Adulthood is dependent upon the *coming to fruition* of a specific section of the brain called *the Pre-Frontal Cortex* (PFC)[43].

Pre-Manhood

According to researchers, the PFC is the section of the human brain responsible for dividing Youth from Adulthood. The PFC is proportionally larger in humans than all other animals. It has also grown proportionally larger in relation to other portions of the human brain over the time humans have purported to have existed on earth. In humans and on average, the PFC continues to grow into the mid-twenties.

The characteristics[44] of an undeveloped PFC are many. Here are just a few:

- Lack of foresight
- Unfocused attention
- Short attention span
- Inappropriate behavior
- Little to no impulse control
- Cannot self-assess realistically
- Little to no delayed gratification
- Strategies and planning are ill-formed
- Lack of weighing behavioral consequences
- Disorganized thinking and problem solving
- Little to no modulation of intense emotions
- Behavior doesn't adjust as situations change
- Inappropriate risk-taking and dangerous behavior
- Inability to consider the future and make predictions
- Short-term rewards take precedence over long-term goals
- Inability to consider multiple streams of complex and challenging information

These are but a few of the many distinguishing characteristics that help identify males who have further growth required of their PFC before reaching manhood. It benefits all coaches and mentors to recognize these characteristics as they support our next generation of males through their Masonic development.

Manhood

Research the PFC enough and you'll learn that it does many functions important to our Masonic path. It is responsible for planning, decision-making, inhibition, social interaction, self-awareness, long-term memory formation, and understanding other people. Included in this, the PFC also watches, supervises, guides, directs and focuses behavior! When mature, it both knows and exhibits wisdom.

If it has not become clear yet, the PFC is responsible for the facilitation of Executive Functions characteristic of mature males. These functions include but are not limited to, *Time Management, Judgment, Impulse Control, Planning, Organization,* and *Critical Thinking.* Furthermore, every last one of these Executive Functions is what Masons should find exemplified by at least one our first three Grand Masters.

What to Do

What do coaches or mentors do with this information? First on the list of things to do should be improving awareness of the telltale characteristics of immaturity. Some are more obvious than others but they are all important to know as you work with others who depend upon your support and guidance.

Once you can recognize and identify specific characteristics, work toward becoming willing to share your awareness with those with whom you work. This does not mean you should though. It merely means that you are positioning yourself to properly assist those current and future Brothers who show signs that they are indeed ready to take steps along the Masonic path and *are ready to hear what you observe about their behavior that can help them.*

Points to Perpend:

1) Should Manhood be determined by maturity and not chronological age?
2) Is the Craft allowing Brothers to pass long before these males have yet to achieve biological manhood?
3) Have you ever allowed a man to enter into Freemasonry or pass from one degree to another without considering his maturity?
4) How would you determine the Maturity of a man if asked to undertake this important endeavor?
5) What are the realized long -term costs to the lodge when males are passed prematurely?

XIII. The Perfect Purpose

*One's
assumptions
permeate
throughout all
that one views.
In return, how
one views
Perfection is
deeply influenced
by these
assumptions.*

Freemason's Rituals allude to activities intended
to perfect men. How men see this *perfection* affects all
that they shall do. More importantly, it affects all that
they shall be.

As shared earlier, you'll encounter Brothers who
have strong opinions about perfection. At some point
in your Fraternal experience, at least one of your
Brothers will proclaim, *"no one is perfect"* while
asserting a very strong belief that *no one will ever be
perfect until they have passed beyond this physical
realm.* Immediately following this proclamation, a
show of support will usually radiate from all who are
present.

It's interesting to view these exchanges. Often
those individuals most adamant to affirm this adage
are the ones least likely to show any significant signs
that they have worked toward improving themselves.
The exchanges are revealing though and they keep
things as they are rather than allow for any true
challenges to their claims.

Counters

Unfortunately, this status quo is antagonistic to Freemasonry's ends and sabotages many a member's forward movement toward betterment. Legitimate Freemasonic practice opens up men to improvement possibilities often never imagined before they entered the Craft. Its Rituals are intended to show men what is entirely possible for them, should they invest themselves toward betterment. Craft activities, those pointed toward by Freemason's Rituals but not the activities of the Rituals themselves, are transformative in nature, but only when applied. Status quo is the very antithesis of this. Improvements to men require corruption of their status quo, in value-adding ways.

There's a perceptually ironic twist in this. Craft activities, designed to bring about order, inundate every Candidate's current order with seemingly overwhelming chaos – at least, to the uninformed mind. *"The storm before the calm"* is an experience that every Candidate goes through at least once especially when they are ill-informed about what it takes to improve themselves. No exacting preparation shall ever prevent this internal whirlwind. It's the natural effect of awakening to the world without and within each and every one of us.

Not understanding fully all that is offered in Ritual aggravates these storms of confusion, especially when the pace of Ritual information delivery is far faster than the manner in which is normally offered in life. Absorption only occurs at the rate governed by each Candidate's ability to comprehend. Far too many Candidates, overwhelmed by these experiential floods, ride them supported only by encouragement to sort them out when these floods recede.

Unfortunately, this sorting out will never occur without further support from within or without.

The typical response to flood aftermaths is to progress to the next flood believing that, one day, understanding will occur inexplicably. It's a rare member who intentionally pauses his progression to understand what he was just offered.

Craft Winnowing

If you have yet to grasp it, the activities alluded to by Ritual which should follow each Degree are designed to continually separate the Fraternal wheat from its chaff. Brothers properly focused take hold of their Working Tools and busy themselves in the business of Working upon their Ashlar. Those remaining overwhelmed by each of their Degree experiences may flounder in an unfocused stupor. They may only engage in rote activities without ever lifting any tool whatsoever, much less applying them. It would do all Candidates well to have coaches and mentors consciously aware that Candidates depend upon sound guidance wrought by working experience at every step of their journey.

One piece of sound guidance involves that word mentioned earlier – *Perfect*. Experienced coaches and mentors know that misunderstanding this word's application to the Speculative activities of Masons shall very likely maneuver them towards hopelessness. The typical Candidate who depends upon others for support in this area might be directed down a path of darkness rather than Light due to its meaning being *high jacked* by many well-meaning Brothers who truly don't know better. It's important for coaches and mentors to convey meaning that provides a viable target. Anything that suggests or conveys an improbability of success is hostile to motivating those Brothers seeking to improve themselves.

There are things that you can do to improve the odds that your support efforts are successful.

Clue Sifting

Cunningly crafted clues to Craft Perfection

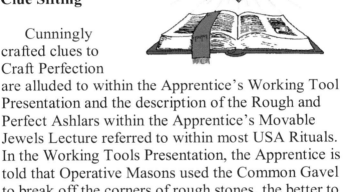

are alluded to within the Apprentice's Working Tool Presentation and the description of the Rough and Perfect Ashlars within the Apprentice's Movable Jewels Lecture referred to within most USA Rituals. In the Working Tools Presentation, the Apprentice is told that Operative Masons used the Common Gavel to break off the corners of rough stones, the better to fit them for the builder's use.[45] In the Movable Jewels description, Apprentices are told that the Perfect Ashlar is a stone made ready by the hands of the workman, to be adjusted by the working tools of the Fellow Craft.[46] Each provides deep thinking Brothers opportunities to see through veils antagonistic to the Light Masonry offers to those who do its Work.

Fitness

From the moment they obligate themselves, Apprentices are involved in a fitness program, or at least they should be if they are to remain true to their intent. Their task is to bring themselves to a suitable state for the Builder's Use. The word used to convey this *suitability* is *Fit* [47] and its roots reflect exactly that: a meaning of "being suitable", "being the right shape" and "being Suited to the circumstance; proper". All Apprentices who make an effort to do the Apprentice Work should understand this fully.

Youth

It is known by many Freemasons and any deep thinking Mason that the Apprentice level of the Craft represents its Youth. In the eyes of the Craft, this is an appropriate classification in that Apprentices have yet to Mature. The activities they each engage in, should they actually do the Work that Ritual directs them toward, are intended to bring them to Maturity at an accelerated rate. The time required by each individual varies. Should each endeavor to engage in these activities fully and completely, fruition is likely to come much sooner than later. Since it is *Character* that indicates completion and not *time served,* coaches and mentors should be careful to avoid assigning completion times to such activities.

Maturity is an ideal word to Characterize the Fitting process offered to Apprentices. Scripture backs this up. Research shows that the multitude of words[48] most commonly and generically translated to the word *perfect* reflect more accurately a general meaning of *Complete, Mature, Healthy, Sound, and Sane* rather than the very often specific and misguided claim of *Flawless.* This is an important distinction and insight toward which coaches and mentors should draw all Apprentices' Work attention and intention.

It should also be pointed out to Apprentices that *Maturity doesn't require flawlessness.* Equal to consider here is that flawlessness doesn't require any maturity whatsoever. Considering whether Maturity or flawlessness has more value to a Builder is an invaluable exercise for all those involved in apprentice activities.

Maturity

Apprentices are asked to use their Working Tools in a directed fashion to break off or divest themselves of what is metaphorically termed *rough corners.* These features of their stone are unnecessary and excessive to what any builder needs. It is a Maturing process that speculatively *shapes* men toward uses more Suited to civil societies.

The symbol of the mature man and Mason that is commonly used within Freemasonry is the *Perfect Ashlar.* It is most unfortunate that a select swath of Brothers insists that such a man and Mason could only exist in death. You'll hear them claim that they shall forever be a Rough Ashlar, never understanding that the Stone to which they refer would never be called *a Rough Ashlar* once any Work has been done upon it. The transitional term used to denote movement from *Rough* to *Perfect* is commonly known to Masons who do the Work.

The Freemasonic Order, however, is silent at the Blue Lodge level on any terms related to ashlars, other than those terms referring to the Rough and Perfect. Those who are uninformed as to Operative lexicon don't know that stone being worked at an Apprentice level is called *a Common Ashlar* also don't realize that they proclaim arrogantly their ignorance and earnestly believe that they have properly characterized

100

themselves. Their claim says to all who know that they have not done any work whatsoever!

Fellow Crafting

The Work that Apprentices do is to Perfect their Ashlars. It is only after this Work is completed that the Fellow Craft tools adjust this Perfect Ashlar. That adjustment is movement only. It involves Raising and Positioning the Perfected Ashlar only and in accordance with the Builder's use. This occurs in both an Operative and a Speculative sense. Specific steps direct that movement and each requires staged Masonic movement.

However, this is performed *only after achieving Maturity.*

Points to Perpend

1) What are synonyms for the word *Perfect?*
2) What is your understanding of the word *Perfect?*
3) What have you and haven't you done to *Perfect* your Ashlar?
4) What must you continue to do to *Perfect?*
5) How differently would this chapter sound to you if you replaced the word *Perfect* with the word "Mature"? How would this change affect your view of the Work?

XIV. A House not made with Hands

No speculative house ever built was assembled using one single stone. Your house requires a multitude of ashlars, all carefully shaped to fit the Builder's Use.

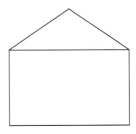

It astounds me when apprentices show up in lodge appropriately attired and other members don't see the immediate reference to a symbolic house wrapped around their waists. The symbol is obvious even to those who have not been trained in symbolism. Yet, there it is, hidden in plain sight.

For those who have studied the Apprentice Ritual, it is fairly easy to draw the connection between the seven virtues (four Cardinal and three Theological) mentioned within the Preston-Webb ritual and the figure apprentices paint upon their waist (properly attired).

This clearly visible reference is like so many other things that are hidden in plain sight. When you have trained your mind to recognize patterns, they tend to leap right out in front of you.

Foundations

You'll undoubtedly reach a point where, if you're building yourself or helping others to do so, you'll realize that there's more than one ashlar involved in these construction efforts. The metaphor initially offered to you by your membership in the Fraternity is surprisingly lacking when you consider all the different things you have to craft within yourself as an Apprentice. Each and every one of these things is a part of your foundation. Yet, each is not the only aspect of your foundation that needs to be built. Crafting each of them as a separate ashlar to completion helps you build your strong foundation. When done well, they join together to become for you a single unified mass upon which you can construct your building.

You might ask yourself, "What exactly are the ashlars you need to perfect to build your foundation?" You would be leading the Masonic pack if you did since most members never get past the single ashlar metaphor.

The ashlars that make up the foundation are grouped into major and minor categories having to do with the following:

1. Values & Priorities
2. Morals, Standards & Boundaries
3. Virtues & Vices
4. Management of Emotions
5. Management of Time.

These areas of focus are the ashlars that lay the foundation for future building so that you don't build upon shifting sands.

Importance

Importance drives the making of a strong foundation. When you don't know what's important, you can't possibly set long run priorities that matter. This is the most crucial thing to determine if you're going to have any success in developing yourself toward Mastery. Without knowing what you value in life, you're going to be redirected as a feather to the winds of the world's distractions.

Importance is founded upon what you value most. You can go through a tremendous amount of soul searching trying to figure out what you value most, but no method is easier than simply examining your life and looking at where you focus your time and energies. When you do this one simple thing you'll see where your time and energies are placed. You'll also see what and who your priorities are. You'll know without any doubt what you most value.

When you realize that you like what you find, then you're on the right path. However, if you're upset at the results of your examination, you might want to ask yourself what results you truly want. It's only after you do this that you can then determine what you have to value most to get results that are more to your liking.

No foundational ashlar will stand the test of time that isn't based upon what you value most and honoring actions that support this.

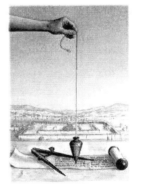

Setting your Plumb

It's of the utmost importance for you as an Apprentice to set your Plumb before commencing any Work. You might ask if this is right since it is not a working tool to which you have been introduced. And you are correct in your assessment. However, you might not realize this, but you're creating a Plumb through your foundation Work. All your actions are internalizing a rule and guide in your great and important undertaking. In a nut shell, setting your Plumb is a metaphor that emphasizes the importance of knowing what you value. This provides you with a standard by which you can guide most of your other activities – *an internal Plumb!*

This Plumb is based upon what you understand and accept to be most important. If you have yet to determine this, please reread that last section and then determine what you value most. Once you have, you're ready to Set your Plumb.

It's one of a few Ashlars you need to perfect in your Foundation before you even begin to lay it.

What Follows

Why is it so important to do this activity up-front? When Apprentices skip over Setting their Plumb, their burnout is inevitable. Applying the Twenty-Four Inch Gauge is founded upon knowing what's important, and what's not important. Without a properly Set Plumb, priorities are not established, much less known. No Mason can use this working tool properly without a Set Plumb. Trying to properly manage one's time without a Set Plumb is insanity.

It is in Setting his Plumb that a Mason determines, establishes and works toward maintaining that which he values most. Until this is done, he does not consciously know what's truly important to him and hence he shall participate unknowingly in multitudes of unimportant and unsupportive activities.

Likewise, the Square will not be true since the entirety of its proper angle is determined by standards that are embraced once he has Set his Plumb. *Without these standards, how would he determine, establish and work toward being moral or virtuous?*

Furthermore, the Level is useless without a Plumb. *How is he going to know how to view and treat others if he has not a Set Plumb?*

Moreover, the compasses require an understanding of what must be circumscribed and why. Without a set plumb to guide that circumscription, his line is not guided by a known and true standard. *Without such guidance, how would he know where and when to draw the line?*

Additionally, without a Set Plumb, his Common Gavel becomes a danger to him. *How is he going to know of what to divest himself without a standard to steadily guide his activities?*

I hope and trust that you can see why it is so important to Set your Plumb and to do so as early in your work as possible.

Morals & Limits

Once you have Set your Plumb by determining what you value most, you'll need to establish what behaviors best honors these values. This is done through *moral investigation* and establishing for yourself what limits you must have in your life that best brings about what you value.

While *morals* are a set of embraced behaviors that increases the probabilities that what you value most will be honored, *standards* and *boundaries* are those limits you must practice to ensure that these values are protected.

Standards, within this context, are those behavioral limits to which you must hold yourself to account to ensure that what you value is honored and respected. They are internal and are acted out externally. They address all intellectual, emotional, physical, temporal and spiritual matters with respect to what you value and the impact your behavior will have upon what you value.

Boundaries, within this context, are those behavioral limits to which you must hold others to account to ensure that what you value is honored and respected. Although they are internal with respect to their origin, they are acted out externally through your behavior with others. They address all intellectual, emotional, physical, temporal and spiritual matters with respect to what you value and the impact your interaction with others will have upon what you value.

All three of these are ashlars of which you will have to perfect should you desire to have a strong and supportive foundation. *I shall expand upon standards and boundaries even further later on in this book.*

Virtues & Vices

Inevitably, perfecting your understanding of your morals lays the foundation for your examination of your behavior. Through this examination, you'll realize all too soon which behaviors support your values and which behaviors dishonor and disrespect these values. The contrast between virtues and vices helps bring further understanding of this most important development issue.

Virtues are strengths. They are those behaviors that act as nurturing resources which we draw upon for all that we want to bring about. Without them, we're weak and are unable to take action with what is needed to bring about success.

Vices are weaknesses. They are also a subcategory of Superfluities that bring about harm to both the one engaging in them and those who are impacted by this engagement. They burden us and keep us from being swift and engaging with what we want to accomplish. Excessiveness is at their core and even a virtue will turn into a vice if practiced in damaging ways.

The key to developing this part of your foundation is to examine your excesses, list them and engage an action plan to bring each excess into a manageable form. As you do this activity, you might notice that you cannot succeed in doing any of this without practicing your virtues as well. It is the practicing of virtue that reduces and eventually eliminates excesses.

Passions & Desires

Emotional management is a tough ashlar to perfect, especially for anyone who avoids talking about emotions. To perfect this ashlar, you must be rigorously honest about what you want and to what lengths you're willing to go to get what you want. The first part of this, what you truly want, is your desires. The second part of this, how far you are willing to go, are your passions.

Desires are based upon what you want. This includes what you avoid as well. When you know what you truly want, you're clear about what your goals are and all the emotions that get wrapped up with those goals.

Passions are based upon what you willingly suffer in order to get what you want. True passion is what you willingly subject yourself, suffering included, to get what you want. No honestly passionate person will ever deny that they would suffer to get what they truly want, even if what they want benefits others.

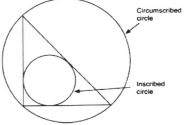

To perfect this foundational ashlar, you must be honest with what you feel. You must know which proper actions you must be engaged in to ensure you get what you want. You must also ensure that your actions will not negatively impact others.

This is why Masons are engaged in subduing and circumscribing. It is a foundational ashlar that once perfected allows for no foundational movements that will shake the house that will eventually be Raised.

Time Management

Lastly, time management requires yet another skill within the Apprentice's foundational structure. Personal time management depends upon specific self-awareness to support its perfection.

What supports this time management perfection?

Self-knowledge! By the time you work upon your personal time management, you should know:

1. *What you value most*
2. *Your limits, personal and social*
3. *What's excessive and harmful*
4. *How to temper excesses and avoid harm*
5. *Your priorities*

These items of self-knowledge act as building blocks to support your time management toward being perfected. Without them shoring up your time management efforts, working within time constraints will likely fail. Time will slip away or be wasted upon things and activities that simply do not matter. Your time will not be used effectively, no matter how efficient you might try to make it.

Time management depends upon these important building blocks. And once they are put into place, you begin to schedule and engage in activities that matter and which support what you value.

On the flip side of this is a clearer understanding of what behavior you must divest yourself. Activities unsupportive of your desired goals will not be engaged in since they are ineffective in bringing about what you are passionate for. And since you have already flanked the time management ashlar with a perfected support block that is strong and unburdened, choices and decisions will be in the direction of what you truly desire.

Heart of the Matter

If you have not already gathered, through this Work you have brought order to the chaos of your heart. This is the focus of the Apprentice Work – *preparing a young male to become a Man and Mason.*

Let's do a quick review.

The most common and accepted response you will get from those trained in Freemasonic proficiencies to the question, "Where were you first Prepared to become a Mason?", is, "In my heart". However, what you will not hear very often is how that preparation occurs and when.

Most men think that this Preparation is done *before* they become members of a Freemasonic Order. And it is understandable how they could be easily led to believe that this was all that this sentence implied.

This question alludes to something much more profound though. If they understand what it takes to actually make a Mason, and not just a member as the Freemasonic term "make" implies[49], then they know that *it is completing the Apprentice Work that prepares their hearts and does so properly.*

Far too many members do not think through the sentence with more diligence and due consideration. If they did, they might come to understand that this sentence more accurately represents the focus of the Apprentice Work which, if left undone, reveals to the world that this Preparation was never started, much less completed.

It also reveals that the person claiming the title is more interested in wearing it than actually doing the rigorous Work required to earn what it represents.

Yet, don't take my word on this. Let's explore this in earnest.

Upon what does the Apprentice Work focus?

If you review what Ritual espouses, it is all about Working upon a man's heart; moving it from chaos to crder. Take some time to review what was written in this chapter and ask yourself the above question again.

Every last one of these activities, presented to you as building blocks that need to be perfected, leads up to and then properly prepares a young man's heart to become a Mason.

As you might have gathered, it's truly not enough to simply *want* to become a Mason or to claim that this first prepared you. One must first properly prepare oneself to become a Mason and that starts with properly preparing one's heart!

With all these building blocks perfected and properly placed, your foundation is firm and ready to support what you must build next – *a Mason!*

Points to Perpend:

1) What have you actually done to properly prepare your heart to do the Work necessary to be a Mason, and not just a member of the order?
2) How has that preparation, or lack of it, impacted your life?
3) What more can you do?

XV. Breaking Ground

The Foundation of each man's Temple
must be Properly Prepared for it to
Suitably Support what is to be Built.

The ground upon which any building is to be erected must be cleared and then strengthened to ensure that what is placed upon it is well supported. Apprentices are best prepared for both the clearing and strengthening by instructors, coaches, and mentors who help them focus upon these activities. This preparation begins with an understanding of the Working Tools and for what they are supposed to be used. Sometimes other Working Tools must be employed by guides so that apprentices accomplish what is necessary to create a much needed strong foundation.

Although the Common Gavel is an appropriate Working Tool for most Apprentices, it's unfortunate that a Pickax is not included for some of these young Brothers! Many of them could benefit from its use in helping make sound the Foundation on which they build. Far too few Brothers ever delve into this very ground. Many simply look upon its surface, assume it is sound and earnestly believe that it shall support strongly what shall ultimately become their future. You'd expect this from Apprentices since it's understood that many only see what is superficially presented and have never been taught how to go beyond this view.

Too soon they often find nothing but woe in every effort to build anything worthwhile due to weak foundations. A Pickax, and proper instruction in its use, would greatly assist many Brothers toward developing a more mature view of betterment.

Will such a working tool ever be included within Blue Lodge Ritual? It is not likely. It's enough to make mention of it to coaches and mentors who can use it to help Candidates probe their building sites when they finally become intent on laying their Foundations.

Coaches and mentors should be mindful of this during Instruction.

Within the United States, many of the Freemasonic Rituals used are legacies of the Preston-Webb effort to standardize Ritual. The Apprentice sections of these Rituals focus upon introducing Candidates to philosophies and principles intended to guide them toward maturity. Included within this introduction are instruments called *Working Tools* that are shown, described, and explained in ways that hopefully support Candidates should they choose to eventually pick them up and use them.

Investment

Divestment

One such Working Tool disclosed within this first Ritual is the Common Gavel. Many Brothers see this Working Tool as a divestment device. When asked about it, they usually quote Ritual verbatim as to its intended use. Unfortunately, much like the tale of the cathedral builders[50] where the first worker replied superficially, too many Brothers do not look beyond the immediate application. Tools should be used with some working knowledge of an end-in-mind.

Superficial

On the surface, the Common Gavel does appear to be a divestment tool. It's said that it represents symbolically the activities that should be embraced, undertaken and completed by all Brothers before they pass on toward other more lofty activities. Apprentices are told that specific superfluous or harmful things (including activities, situations, and people) should be both let go of and not pursued any more. Unfortunately for Apprentices, when not thought through deeply, only the surface is focused upon. However, when thought out, and when investigated further by Candidates, it soon becomes clear to them that much more is required when wielding this Tool.

Knowing this, coaches and mentors should use the intent of this Tool to communicate to Candidates that there is far more than divestment going on when this Working Tool is brandished.

Instructors should encourage Candidates to go beyond the Superficial. The mechanics implied by such divestment also require the exact opposite. This means, to *divest,* one must also *invest,* not in that which is divested, but in four Maturity supporting areas:

1. new Understandings
2. new Beliefs
3. new Attitudes
4. new Behaviors.

No true divestment occurs without true Investment on the part of the divesting person involved. To help develop Candidate maturity, coaches and mentors should encourage in-depth discourse along these lines.

Get Picky

The four maturity supporting areas of investment also require *rigorous investigation* and *utter honesty*. When these two are not present, all outcomes are suspect and lean toward corruption either directly or indirectly. When both are present and fully functioning as supports for the investments, they improve outcomes tremendously.

This is where Pickaxes lend some great value to Apprentices and tend toward cultivating maturity. While the Common Gavel is viewed and used upon the superficial aspects of Ashlars to divest their surfaces of all unnecessary excess, the Pickax requires its users to break through surfaces and invites them to investigate what exists below the surface, especially when it involves their Foundation!

To ensure that Candidates break ground for any new building efforts, coaches and mentors should become familiar with respectful and potent probing techniques that they can offer when asked and when necessary.

However, until Brothers are ready to break through the superficial veils, they will not be ready to discover the sources of their understandings, beliefs, attitudes and behavior. They will continue to focus upon only the symptoms that arise within their lives and not the causes of those symptoms. Consequently, their Foundations will likely never be suitable for the builder's use.

This being said, you can still make significant progress though by continually directing their attention to the Common Gavel. You can show how it is symbolic for the virtues mentioned within the First Degree that they must wield endlessly within themselves to ensure that vices and superfluities are divested. You can invite them to discuss at length how exercising specific virtues would diminish and even eliminate specific vices and superfluities. In doing so, you would be using the discourse to invite them to use it eventually and successfully.

As an instructor, coach or mentor to this next generation of Brothers, you are charged with assisting them in cultivating their maturity *beyond the superficial!*

Divestment requires investment; Investment requires investigation. Proper investigatory tools are necessary! Make sure your Candidates know what they can and should be used for and how to use them successfully!

Points to Perpend:

1) What investments have you made to Better your Understandings, Beliefs, Attitudes and Behaviors?
2) What steps have you already taken to ensure that these investments paid off?
3) What further investments have you yet to make?
4) What steps must you Invest in to ensure that these further investments occur?
5) What must you invest to make sure the next generation of members is properly supported toward maturity?

XVI. Perfect Restrictions

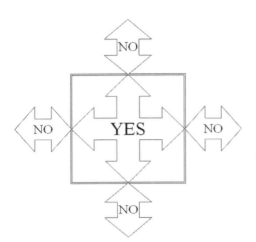

Mastery demands Brothers to develop Maturity within themselves. Wisdom reveals that Maturity cannot, shall not and will not be handed down from one generation to another.

With entry into the Craft, Candidates are offered unique opportunities to learn, develop, and practice principles that are long known to create better lives. Although many men have been given these opportunities, not enough of them realize the foundation these opportunities make effort to lay.

If you haven't considered that the Craft's end is to better males by first maturing them, you might have missed some serious thought-provoking opportunities. Pause and ask yourself *why this specific end?* You might find that it is so that these Brothers can, shall and will eventually take this maturity and travel, work, earn, support and contribute Masterfully. None of this can be done immaturely with any degree of consistent success.

Freemasonry's Ritual cleverly directs Brothers toward a maturing process. The progression they must go through toward maturity is clearly spelled out within its Degrees. Freemasons know that the First Degree denotes what it takes to move a youthful male to manhood – *no matter what*

age he starts the process! The Second Degree denotes what it takes to move a man from manhood to mastery. The Third Degree prepares a man for what is to eventually come – *Age* – if he is fortunate to live long enough to accomplish this.

There is no message given more clearly or concisely to those who embrace the Craft than the importance of maturing. All else, every speculation, elaboration, and confabulation, are mere supporting props to this all-important main theme.

An important first step toward maturity is making and keeping commitments. This entails establishing and maintaining clearly defined standards and boundaries. One specific entry-level standard is keeping inviolate within one's chest specific knowledge[51]. Another one involves circumscription. A third is keeping within due bounds[52]. Each of them exemplifies standards of behavior that must exist and be honored for maturity to come to fruition. Without these standards, all hope for maturity withers.

Boundaries are different though. In the Masonic realm, one specific example of a boundary would be how one goes about responding to questions about

Freemasonic Light, especially when asked by someone who clearly and without question has no right to it. Of course, those who have the right to it are treated much differently.

Limits

As a Master Mason, you have hopefully progressed toward Maturity yourself. If you have succeeded, you might also be making effort to aid in the maturing of other Brothers who have yet to gain suitable Mastery. To help them, you must provide them with opportunities to test and develop their judgments until perfected.

Establishing standards and boundaries is one way to provide these opportunities to them. By offering something that requires specific Restrictions, it challenges those taking these offers to exercise good judgment in keeping commitments.

If you have not clearly voiced it before, standards and boundaries are about selective restrictions that promote well-being and enrichment. Standards and boundaries are not served well without these selective restrictions. These restrictions require the exercising of good and sound discernment, something that is required should there be any hope of eventually developing wisdom. Having Brothers commit to developing and practicing discernment assists them toward developing maturity.

Standards

It is valuable to have a working definition of *standards* when you work with others in assisting them toward establishing and maintaining new personal operating parameters. Such working definitions help in bringing about a better understanding. From bettered understandings come abilities to recognize when standards are there, and when they are missing. Such knowledge also aids in diagnosing when standards have not been properly established or maintained.

What is a working definition for *standards? They are those limits to which a mature man holds himself to account.* They are his operating parameters[53] when it comes to self. A mature man is responsible for both establishing and maintaining worthwhile and life-enriching standards. No one else should do this for the man. To have anyone else do this for him would classify him as immature.

Of course, Apprentices are given standards to operate by because they are considered youths. They have yet to mature enough to set their own standards and hence they are provided those that should assist them toward maturity. Should they shirk their responsibility to honor these standards and not do the Work to ensure that these standards are established and maintained, they shall not bring about the maturity that these standards help cultivate.

Boundaries

It is also valuable to have a working definition of *boundaries* when you work with others in assisting them toward establishing and maintaining new social operating parameters. Such working definitions help in bringing about better understanding. From a bettered understanding come abilities to recognize when boundaries are there, and when they are missing. Such knowledge also aids in diagnosing when boundaries have not been properly established or maintained.

What is a working definition for boundaries? *They are those limits to which a man holds others to account.* They are his operating parameters when it comes to how he conducts himself with others. A mature man is responsible for both establishing and maintaining worthwhile and life-enriching boundaries. No one else should do this for the man. To have anyone else do this for him would classify him as immature.

Of course, Apprentices are given boundaries to operate by because they are considered immature. They have yet to mature enough to set their own boundaries and hence they are provided those that should assist them toward maturity. Should they shirk their responsibility to honor these boundaries and not do the work to ensure that these boundaries are established and maintained, they shall not bring about the maturity that these boundaries help cultivate.

Further Work

There are many standards and boundaries that are offered to the youth of the Craft, especially when they first enter. These standards and boundaries are right there within Ritual and they are not veiled in any way. As coaches and mentors, it behooves you to ask the next generation of Craft Brothers what standards and boundaries they remember from their Ritual experience. You might want to start the conversation by asking them what they know about standards and boundaries. They might just surprise you *once you clarify definitions and provide them with an example or two*.

Be ready for some challenging discourse should you truly desire to assist them in maturing. The insights and questions

that you share should stimulate their thinking. These should also help develop their discernment quicker than had you not involved them in any challenge other than rote learning. Properly preparing for this important task might also require that you reevaluate and possibly work upon your own maturity.

If maturing the next generation is important to you, then you will be motivated to do the right thing and not just the *rite* thing. If it is not, you will continue to do what many Brothers before you have done and merely pass down only what was *handed to you* and not help others cultivate what was *developed by you*.

Should you be an effective coach or mentor to this next generation of Brothers, you have an important task ahead of you and this task should not be taken lightly. It's been said many times that Apprentices are the life's blood of the Fraternity. Keep in mind that *good, honest and thoughtful discourse is its oxygen!* Come properly prepared for it and don't leave anyone suffocating or gasping for air.

Here are some conversation kickers that you can use to help bring about quicker development:

Circumscribing specific behaviors, divesting other behaviors and cultivating different behaviors related to the standards and boundaries offered by Ritual to Craft youth.

1. Ask them what these behaviors are.
2. Ask them what challenges they must face in establishing new behaviors, in stopping other behaviors and in limiting specific behaviors.
3. Ask them how important they think these actions are to them and others.
4. Ask them how their behaviors reflect their seriousness and commitment to the Craft and themselves.

Then brace yourself for some tremendous discourse!

Points to Perpend:

1) How do you define standards and how do you define boundaries?
2) What distinguishes standards from boundaries and what standards & boundaries can you identify within Ritual?
3) What new standards & boundaries have you established and maintained since joining the Craft?

XVII. Perfect Discourse

If Apprentices are the life's blood of the Fraternity, then Discourse is its oxygen!

When you earnestly engage in educational efforts, especially those involving young minds, you quickly  learn methods of bringing forth their best thoughts. This is an absolute must since those you engage may have preconceived notions, attitudes and behaviors that prevent forward progress. The more you engage yourself in learning what works best, the apter you are to assist others toward their goals.

There is one method that has a proven track record for producing superior results. This technique is *The Socratic Method* so wonderfully immortalized by Plato. It is one of the most powerful and quickest ways to improve a man through discourse. As rendered by Plato in his dialogs, the interaction between two or more men can sharpen those involved and do so in lasting ways, as steel sharpens steel to a fine edge. It's a gentle and loving approach, filled with respectful exchanges, loving folly and playfulness at times and blunt thought-provoking statements, all designed to foster enlightenment for those who engage in it.

The process is straight forward. Ask him a question or ask if he has any questions. Get him involved in voicing his opinions and his interests. Challenge him to back up what he says with facts and figures or to do his own research. It matters not how you start. What matters most is to engage him with both your heart and your mind.

What is to follow is an example of such an engagement. The subject is apprenticeship and, more specifically, when does apprenticeship clearly end.

The Forever Apprentice

Brother: Coach, I've seen many times when members of the organization put forth to others that they may be wearing the title of a Master Mason, but they will always be an apprentice "because they still have a lot to learn".

Coach: Yes. I've seen that more times than I can remember.

Brother: And what's more, they take it one step further.

Coach: Further!

Brother: Yes!.. and claim anyone who is learning is still an Apprentice.

Coach: Yes. I've heard that also. They usually add that anyone who doesn't see themselves as an Apprentice, regardless of title, is likely not learning a thing.

Brother: Exactly!

Coach: If you stick around long enough, you'll encounter members who claim quite proudly that they are Apprentices, even though they wear titles that clearly denote that the organization has moved them past this stage of development.

Thoughts

Brother: What are your thoughts about these Brothers claiming to be Apprentices too?

Coach: It's pretentious and shows the Brother doesn't fully understand what Apprentice Work focuses upon.

Brother: Wow Coach. Don't hold back. Tell me what you *really* think.

Coach: <chuckle> What?! Not enough?

Brother: Well, you usually start out responding to my question with your own line of questions.

Coach: And?

Brother: You cut to the punch line on this one.

Coach: It's not rocket science my Brother.

Brother: Yes, but that's it? You're not going to get into it? No gentle build-up to a blunt statement?

Coach: What's there to say Brother? The claim is not only a façade, it also exudes false modesty – a terrible illusion to put in front of those *who want better* and *who are working toward it.* It's also an affront to those *who do know better.*

Bread Crumb Techniques

Brother: Okay. You see right there? You did it again.

Coach: Did what again?

Brother: You've planted the bread crumbs right in front of me to get me to go down another rabbit hole with you.

Coach: Am I?

Brother: You sure are.

Coach: How's that?

Brother: I know you. We've been here before. You want me to ask you about all your statements. This is even worse than asking me a series of questions.

Coach: Worse? Brother, you know, we really don't *have* to go there.

Brother: No. That's wrong, Coach. We now have to go there *and you know it.*

Coach: Well, okay, if you insist.

Brother: I do.

Going In

Coach: So, where do you want to start?

Brother: Let's start with your statement about the claim being "pretentious".

Coach: Okay.

Brother: Isn't that like saying that they're attempting to impress others by affecting greater importance on what they claim than what's actually possessed.

Coach: Yes.

Brother: But that doesn't make any sense.

Coach: Really? How so?

Brother: Wouldn't it be just the opposite?

Coach: Would you please explain?

Brother: Apprenticeship is not more important as Mastery to a Master.

Coach: Yes, and?

Brother: By implying through

their claim that it's more important, they are claiming lesser title and lesser being than they actually are.

Coach: Yes. They are doing just that, especially when they truly did the Work to earn the title they proudly, and hopefully rightfully, wear.

Brother: I don't understand this.

Coach: And neither do those who falsely claim to be an Apprentice when they wear the title of Fellow or Master if they did the Work. By the way, this is also in line with my false humility statement.

Brother: But I want to understand it. Would you lead me through it, please?

Coach: Sure. They are claiming they are less than they actually are and are implying this lesser state is more important. This is all under the pretense that they are still learning.

Twists

Brother: Wow! That's pretty convoluted.

Coach: Yes it is. And they get away with this claim most of the time.

Brother: Why?

Coach: Because it's also implying that you're less important than them if you don't buy into their illusion of false modesty and the false premise that to continue to learn, you must be an Apprentice.

Brother: That's a mind game, isn't it?

Coach: Of course it is, and it's a heart game as well.

Brother: A heart game?

Coach: Yes. They're playing on your shame and fear.

Brother: My shame and fear? I don't understand.

Coach: They're assuming that you'll feel ashamed enough to claim the same, even though you aren't what they claim they are. All of this is banking on an additional belief that when you don't claim the same, they might confront you and embarrass you. It's a contrived set-up, you sense this fear and they play on it as well.

Brother: Okay, that's unbelievably manipulative as well.

Coach: Indeed. It's an immature ego[54] trip. And anyone who has any misgivings about the title they rightfully earned may feel ashamed to say anything against this Apprentice claim for fear of being attacked and shown to be arrogant or less than for doing so.

Brother: Yikes!

Coach: Why so surprised?

Brother: It's startling!

Coach: It is! And when you have done the Apprentice Work you are less likely to fall for emotional manipulation.

Brother: Why's that?

Coach: You've worked on your heart and know when it's being yanked around. What's more, if you have done the Fellow Craft Work, you recognize instantly the sophistry that's being employed to persuade you into compliance.

Brother: The Work helps you recognize all this?

Coach: It does indeed. Part of the reason for doing the Work is to recognize these patterns and know how to deal with them accordingly.

Brother: Okay. So, males who have yet to do this Work won't recognize the patterns. They would experience them as chaos and not know what to do to bring things back into order.

Coach: Yes! The simple fact is this: when you have done the Work and earned the titles appropriately, you're mature and no longer the inexperienced youth you were previously. It transforms you! Furthermore, Fellow Crafts who have done the Apprentice Work won't buy into emotional manipulation in the least; *they know better.*

The Goal

Brother: Agreed. But do you think anyone ever stops doing the Apprentice or Fellow Craft work?

Coach: Why do you assume this?

Brother: It's never perfected.

Coach: I don't think this for a minute.

Brother: Why?

Coach: You're using the word *perfect* to denote *flawlessness.* Ritual does not agree with you in this use.

Brother: How so?

Coach: Perfecting, as in "brought to flawlessness" has nothing to do with earning the title. Maturing enough to have the title does.

Brother: Maturing rather than flawlessness?

Coach: Yes. Maturing is the goal. The Work we do was never about being Flawless; *it was always about Maturing.*

Proper Mindsets

Brother: Please explain this.

Coach: Sure. You can't be a suitable Fellow Craft until you bring order to the chaos of your heart. This requires maturing from Youth to Manhood.

Brother: That's the Apprentice Work, right?

Coach: Yes! You bring order to the chaos of your heart by completing the Apprentice Work enough to do just that. When you're done, you've matured into Manhood.

Brother: But what if there are storms that cause heart chaos afterward?

Coach: You mean to ask, "Will you be unable to deal with them?"

Brother: Yes!

Coach: When you have done your Work you will. And you will do so maturely if you already laid the foundation and matured.

Brother: What about Master Masons?

Coach: Likewise, you cannot be a valid Master Mason until you bring order to the chaos of both your heart and your head, and bring each into alignment with each other.

Brother: Both?

Coach: Of course! The two being ordered and in alignment is what makes you suitable to be a Master Mason.

Brother: How do you have them both ordered?

Coach: You do that by completing the Apprentice and Fellow Craft Work enough to do just that.

Future Storms

Brother: What about the storms occurring afterward? Will you be unable to deal with them maturely?

Coach: Of course, when you have completed your Apprentice and Fellow Craft Work you will. In other words, you deal with life at a Master's level, not at an Apprentice or Fellow Craft level. But you appear to think that just because there are storms messing with the order of either your head or heart, that somehow this raises a question as to your Fellow Craft or Master's qualifications... right?

Brother: Exactly!

Coach: Brother, life brings forth storms that mess with our well-ordered minds and hearts all the time.

Brother: Yes it does just that!

Coach: When you bring order to your head and heart, you have learned how to do it and then do it as a matter of being.

Brother: Because it's now *who you are?*

Coach: Yes! Exactly!

Brother: Okay. And when storms hit, you have the skills well-developed to handle the chaos at a Master's level?

Coach: Yes!

Brother: Okay, I understand it now.

Coach: Good! Give it back to me then.

Brother: Sure. Because you've matured and gained experience, you're able to deal with what life throws at you more effectively, efficiently and maturely than someone with less maturity, experience and skill development.

Coach: You got it! Kudos!

Testing

Brother: But isn't it like passing an exam?

Coach: How so?

Brother: Doing the work "enough" to get a pass; in other words, getting that pass or title.

Coach: Meaning?

Brother: There is still *so much else* to be learned about the degree.

Coach: Sure, but *it's not* about learning more about any degree.

Brother: It's not?

Coach: Of course not. It's about moving from Youth to Manhood and then from Manhood to Age. The degrees only point this out.

Brother: But much more work needs to be done to perpetuate and prolong the stability of that "order from chaos".

Coach: As I said before, the Work will never prevent life's storms. There is always chaos to bring to order.

Brother: Yes, but when a Brother is doing Apprentice Work, he doesn't need Fellow Craft or Master's skills to progress through it. Similarly, he doesn't need a Master's skills to continue with the Fellow Craft study or Work.

Coach: Only when you're looking at it as an assembly line movement from one title to another. However, this is not an assembly line situation. These are mental stages of development.

Brother: How's that?

Coach: Apprentices are Youths. They are by their very nature immature. They deal with life and its storms from an immature point of view. The

Apprentice Work is there to help them Mature and in doing it, it provides vital skill development to handle chaos effectively *when it occurs* and not *if it occurs*.

Brother: Okay.

Coach: But more importantly, the Work helps them create a life of order which, when chaos occurs, they recognize it more readily and know from experience how to bring it back into order. When the Work doesn't mature them, then the Work is incomplete. When the Work matures them, then the Work *is* complete. Get it?

Stages

Brother: Okay. I mean, I think so. What about Fellow Crafts?

Coach: Fellow Crafts are mature, also known as "adult", males; we refer to them as "men". They are by their very nature mature in their outlook, manner and being. They deal with life from a mature point of view and they have the life skill development to handle chaos when it occurs. If they didn't, they would be Apprentices still.

Brother: So, what does their Work do for them?

Coach: It cultivates their minds so that they can better help bring order to the world around them, make sense of things that bewilder others who have not done the Work and prepare themselves for serious studies of things that are beyond most people.

Brother: Like?

Coach: Thoughts, writings, and discourses presenting, discussing and examining theological and philosophical issues.

Brother: Interesting. What about Masters?

Coach: Masters are men with experience. They are by their very nature both mature and experienced with skills. They deal effectively with life from a mature and experienced point of view. If they didn't, they would not be Masters.

Context is Important

Brother: I don't disagree, but I still think a "youth" can do the Apprentice work so much further than "enough", without necessarily becoming a Fellow Craft or Master.

Coach: I agree. One can do the Work and never mature; doing the Work is no guarantee of maturity. Not doing the Work though is a guarantee that maturity will never occur.

Brother: But don't we sometimes need to become childlike to see the Light?

Coach: Sometimes yes, especially when it comes to Faith. However, context is important here.

Brother: How so?

Coach: One can become childlike and in those times it doesn't mean that *we become children again,* or in this case Apprentices.

Brother: Ah! So you're saying that this is a classic example of a straw man argument.

Coach: Yes. But, just for clarity, please explain it if you would.

Brother: Sure. By claiming one must be childlike is akin to becoming a child again, the analogy is overlaid to support the "being an apprentice" again claim when learning something new.

Coach: And?

Brother: It is setting up a false analogy. One doesn't become a child again to assume childlike qualities. And learning anything new does not make one an apprentice again.

Coach: Agreed!

Brother: I had not considered this before.

Coach: That's one of the reasons for studying Logic. You learn to spot logical fallacies.

Brother: That's why we are taught to learn them.

Coach: That's why we're *instructed* to learn them, *not taught*.

Brother: *We're not taught?* Wait! I thought ritual says we *are taught*.

Coach: Yes, it does say we are "taught" and it does use that term several times. However, there is a huge difference between being *told* to do something and being *taught* how to do something. They are two entirely different things.

Brother: Okay, let me take it from here.

Coach: Sure.

Brother: The former is instruction; being informed. The latter is transforming with guaranteed results.

Coach: Yes. This goes back to understanding terms within context.

Brother: So, *you must comprehend the meaning of the term "are taught" within the context it's offered to you for you to grasp its intent.*

Coach: And to take it out of this context and assume it means the same thing is to mislead.

Brother: In this case, *are taught* means *are told what to do.* Yikes! I agree! You're right! I see what you are saying and you're spot on.

Coach: Thanks.

Brother: How do we apply this to the Work?

Coach: I'm glad you brought this back around. Apprentice Work *prepares us to learn.* In *doing* the Apprentice Work, we are strengthened by virtues and we're released from unnecessary burdens, vices & superfluities, which get in the way of learning.

Brother: This makes sense. Are you saying it's more difficult to learn as an Apprentice than as a Fellow Craft or Master?

Coach: That's exactly what I am saying!

Brother: So, a weak male, burdened with unnecessary excess, is not going to learn as well as a strong male who is free from unnecessary distractions.

Coach: Yes!

Brother: This understanding didn't come to me until after we started talking about this.

Coach: You are not alone in this.

Brother: I'm not?

Coach: You are not. Not many Brothers have thought this through.

Brother: What about the Fellow Craft?

Coach: That Work helps us *learn how to learn.* In doing so, it lays the pathways within our mind for easier learning of those things which would perplex the less trained and disordered mind.

Brother: So, learning how to learn trains the mind to recognize things that untrained minds would find difficult to grasp?

Coach: And it provides to that mind tools and processes to deal with things that have already been learned by others.

Brother: Thus reducing the learning curve on things already explored?

Coach: Yes!

Brother: Wow! I had not thought about it that way.

Coach: And now?

Brother: It's clear that many Brothers have yet to consider what this Work does for the hearts and minds of those who do it. And this included me until now.

State of Mind

Coach: Yes. I agree. My point is this. We complete the Apprentice Work when we have a mature heart and are ready for cultivating a Fellow Craft state of mind; that is, a mature mind that is trained to learn further. Likewise, we complete the Fellow Craft Work when we have both a mature heart and mind and are ready to cultivate a Master's state of mind; that is, mature and experienced. The minutia of the Work itself is to get us to the next level of maturity, experience and skill level.

Brother: So, *it's not about the Work; it's about what the Work transforms within us that matters most!*

Coach: *Absolutely!*

Brother: But there is a term in Zen Buddhism which means "beginner's mind".

Coach: Okay. Where are you going with this?

Brother: It refers to having an attitude of openness, eagerness, and lack of preconceptions when studying a subject, even when studying at an advanced level, just as a beginner in that subject would. Like an Apprentice.

Coach: And?

Brother: The Zen teacher Shunryu Suzuki, says the following about the beginner's mind, "In the beginner's mind there are many possibilities, in the expert's mind there are few."

Coach: Yes. Please continue.

Brother: As a leader, if you assume an attitude of a beginner and believe something can be learned from everyone you encounter, you begin to experience the power of other positive leadership qualities.

Not a Beginner

Coach: "If" being the operative term.

Brother: Of course, but what do you say to that "if"?

Coach: As a leader, you are *not* a beginner. You're an *experienced mature player* and you are foolish to not play the role at that level. That is the reason you were put in the position of leader. Experienced leaders look for an opportunity to learn to become better leaders. But, in truth, they are not beginners in doing so. They have *prepared themselves to learn* and they have *learned how to learn* through doing the First and Second Degree Work respectively. These are not achievements of a beginner and a leader doesn't feign a lesser role or title, especially when all who look up to him that have any self-respect would think less of him for his false and faked modesty.

Brother: But what about all the possibilities that could be considered that an expert's mind dismisses.

Coach: What about them?

Brother: Shouldn't the expert consider them?

Coach: Only when the possibilities are appropriate to the end-in-mind. The expert, if cultivated properly, has already considered the many possibilities.

Brother: And?

Coach: And the expert knows which possibilities work and which ones either don't work or which require more resources to accomplish an end then would be wise to pursue.

Brother: So, having an expert mind doesn't mean you dismiss the awareness of many possibilities…

Coach: Yes, the expert mind is already experienced in considering the many possibilities, once being an Apprentice, and dismisses those possibilities that are either ineffective or less efficient. That's the whole point of expertise! It is brought about by experience!

Brother: Okay. So what you are saying is when a Fellow Craft or Master is learning new stuff he is merely "assuming" the role of an Apprentice, not "being" an Apprentice?

Coach: No. I am saying that when you are a Fellow Craft, you have the Fellow Craft state of heart and mind and expertise that backs them up. Likewise, when you are a Master, you have the Master's state of heart and mind. You learn at the level of your heart and mind. This is why there are few possibilities for an experienced mind. Experts have already tried or considered these many possibilities. In doing so, they have found the ones that work best.

Brother: So, what the Zen teacher was saying was not that the expert mind was limited in what it sees. It is that the expert mind is experienced in what it sees.

Coach: Exactly. Seeing more possibilities is not always a good thing; especially when those possibilities are known to be absolute wastes of time.

Brother: Got it! The Zen statement is too often taken that experts are narrow-minded rather than communicating the truth: *Beginner minds have yet* *to understand what works due to lack of extensive experience. A beginner, through lack of experience, has yet to become an authority!*

Coach: An Authority?

Brother: Yes, a person with extensive or specialized knowledge about a subject; an expert.

Who's Your Daddy?

Coach: Agreed! Becoming a mature male who has learned how to learn sets you up to be your own authority, over yourself not others.

Brother: Please say more about this.

Coach: Sure. As a Master Mason, I have no desire for any authority other than my own and that of God in

my life. I've learned to see past outward distinction, but not be foolish enough to ignore them. I'm not alone in this either.

Brother: You're not?

Coach: I'm not. I am part of an organization of like-minded and like-hearted souls. We call each other "Brothers" within the fraternity, rather than "Fathers" or any other label that denotes we are beholden to a Father Figure. We are our own men, mature in that right and we seek the company of the same.

Brother: Ah! That's why we're known as "widow's sons".

Coach: Exactly!

Brother: But you are dependent upon superiors still?

Coach: I can be, when appropriate to my ends-in-mind. More importantly though is that I am *appropriately interdependent* with the right superiors, because I have become independent through my Work. I realize and know the benefits of working with others in harmony. Those with whom I work believe as I, and *we have no father save the One True God.*

Brother: Wow! That's deep.

Full Circle

Coach: So, claiming you are at a lower state of heart and mind than you actually are, or at least should be, is false humility; it's pretentious and beneath you.

Brother: Okay, I see what you are saying and I agree. I truly appreciate you walking through this with me.

Coach: And I appreciate you walking beside me in this activity. It means a lot to me.

Brother: How so?

Coach: It keeps me sharp.

Brother: Like steel sharpening steel?

Coach: Indeed! Behold!...

Brother: ...How good and pleasant it is...

Coach: ...for Brothers to dwell in unity.

Brother: *Perfect!*

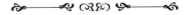

XVIII. Completing One's Foundation

The Attributes that <u>Contribute to</u> and are <u>Indicative of</u> Maturity, Completion and Wholeness are pointed toward by the Entered Apprentice Degree.

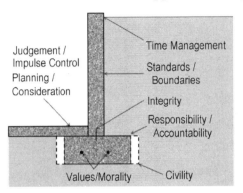

Judgement / Impulse Control Planning / Consideration

Time Management

Standards / Boundaries

Integrity

Responsibility / Accountability

Values/Morality   Civility

The answer to what the Perfect Ashlar is can be found within Ritual. Obtaining the answer however requires you to carefully examine the Development Work that is required during an actual suitable Apprenticeship as indicated by what is revealed by ritual.

The key once again is focusing upon what helps Transform Youths to Adults. Each aspect of development requires specific skills that indicate maturity. Keep in mind that it is not any singular skill that is an indication. It is a group of skills all working in harmony that reveals the person possessing them to be mature. Those skills are what lay the foundation for the building that will eventually be built should the builder continue applying himself toward those ends.

If your Apprenticeship did not entail the following Skill Development, it's a clear indication that you were cheated and misled into thinking that you had matured enough to progress.

1. **Integrity**

   This is pointed out by the *promises* the Candidates made during their obligation. Integrity demands we adhere to the words we put forth, tempering them at every point to ensure that we don't say anything that cannot be supported. Being true to one's Word is a strong indication of maturity.

2. **Proper Impulse Control**

   This is pointed out by the Virtue *Temperance* as revealed through Ritual. Proper impulse control requires one to think through one's choices, decisions and actions before they are implemented to ensure that they are supportive of one's proper goals. Properly balancing one's choices and acting temperately is a strong indication of maturity.

3. **Proper Judgment & Critical Thinking**

   This is pointed out by the Virtues *Prudence* and *Justice* as revealed during Ritual. Proper judgment and critical thinking require letting go of choices, decisions, and actions that do not support one's desired ends. Proper judgment is among one of the strongest indications of maturity.

4. **Proper Morality**

   This is pointed out by the *Plumb, Square, Level, and Volume of Sacred Law* as revealed during Ritual. Proper morality requires that you be a person who takes no action out of line with what you profess to be sacred. Being upright and unbiased, virtuous, fair and pious in all one's worldly and spiritual engagements are all strong indications of maturity.

5. **Proper Standards and Boundaries**

This is pointed out by the *Compasses, Cable-Tow, and Volume of Sacred Law* as revealed during ritual. Proper standards and boundaries require unwavering respect and adherence to personal and social limits. Ensure that one properly limits one's passions and desires to ensure that they do not interfere with one's plans and the plans of others are strong indications of maturity.

6. **Proper Consideration and Civility**

This is pointed out by the *Level, Compasses, and Volume of Sacred Law* as revealed during Ritual. Proper consideration and civility demand one to adhere to an unwavering social code of conduct. Respect in the form of due consideration and civility toward others are strong indications of maturity.

7. **Proper Time Management**

This is pointed out by the *Twenty-Four Inch Gauge* and the concepts and ideals offered to Candidates during its presentation. Proper time management requires letting go of wasteful actions, activities, and focuses, as indicated by the need to divest vices and superfluities. Managing ones time, setting priorities and putting what's and who's most important first are all strong indications of maturity.

8. **Proper Planning & Organizing**

This is pointed out by one of three jewels, the Trestle-board, revealed during Ritual. Proper planning and organizing require one to engage in forward thinking to ensure that outcomes are as desired. The plans and designs drawn upon it show their proper use and are strong indications of maturity.

9. **Proper Responsibility**

This is pointed out by the Cable Tow as revealed by Ritual. Proper responsibility requires taking on only those tasks suited toward one's desired ends. Ensuring that one's obligations to one's personal life properly limit one's engagements outside is a strong indication of maturity.

10. **Proper Accountability**

This is pointed out by the *Compasses and Volume of Sacred Laws* revealed by Ritual. Proper accountability requires one to accept the outcomes one creates by virtue of the position one accepts. Holding oneself to account for the results of choices, decisions, actions and inactions are all strong indications of maturity.

This list appears in no particular order and the list is not complete. *As it is presented, it shows a natural progression from giving and being true to one's word to being accountable for the word that one gives.* Along the way from one to the other are many skills necessary to support the two, preventing them from ever being severed in twain.

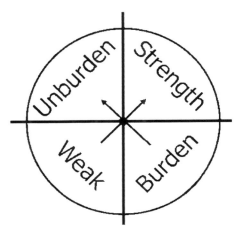

It is important to also note the whole of the Apprentice Work is to both Build Strength and Provide Relief by Unburdening the Apprentice of anything that is unnecessary and harmful to what the Apprentice professes he wants to bring about for himself. This is the foundation from which the future member is to build upon.

It should also be clear that the skills required to bring each of these about all contribute to the maturity of the one mastering them.

By mastering them, one masters oneself. By mastering one's self, what is to come becomes well-supported.

Points to Perpend:

1) Have you truly Received Proper Support to Properly Mature?
2) How skillful would you rate yourself if pressed to do a personal assessment indicating maturity?
3) What aspects are missing from your skills that prevent you from being an individual strong in his maturity?

XIX.   A Secret about Secrets

You might be asking yourself at this point, "How do I get members to take upon themselves such a monumental task as Maturing?"

The answer to this is that you don't. This is self-directed Work. Candidates must want and seek this Work for themselves.

That being said, locked away in the secluded regions of Masonic development is a secret known to very few. It is one of the best-kept secrets within the Freemasonic Order. Although it is a secret, it is still planted within each Candidate every single time he goes through a degree.

That secret is received as a Trojan horse to some and a cornucopia to others. It doesn't matter how it is experienced though. The end result is the same for all. Those who receive it have endless opportunities to transform themselves as a result of possessing it.

You might be scratching your head at this point, trying to figure out what is being alluded to here. And this perhaps is the reason I introduced this chapter's topic in this manner. I wanted to have you get curious about something that all Candidates and their instructors, coaches, and mentors should know.

The Secret

There's a technique used to help bring about maturity in those who are ready for it. It's right there in Ritual! That technique is giving an immature individual something that requires taking on mature responsibility. When the individual seriously takes on

148

that responsibility, their thinking and actions will change in line with that burden.

One of the simplest of responsibilities Ritual offers to Candidates is taking on secrets. Heaped upon that responsibility are conditions in which that secret can and should be shared.

There are benefits to sharing and keeping secrets. It costs nothing for the individual sharing that secret, if the secret is kept. It is extremely costly for those who don't. Discussing the costs and benefits of keeping secrets is a great way to draw Candidate's attention to things they might not have considered. It also helps Candidates develop appreciation for individuals who remain true to their word for in doing so trust is developed between all involved.

Candidates take on many responsibilities several times during the Blue Lodge experience. All of these responsibilities involve acting in mature manners. Candidates promise that they will do specific things that, when followed through upon, will better and mature them as males. Part of this is to keep certain things secret from those who have yet to do the same.

Individuals seeking to mature will respect and adhere to their words. Those who struggle to do so will be seen by others as not ready to progress toward mature activities.

Points to Perpend:

1) How can you broach the topic of secrecy with your Candidates?
2) What responsibilities are shared within Ritual that are clear opportunities for maturing activities?
3) What are the obvious costs to Candidates for not being true to their words?

XX. Perfect Connections

*Jacob's Ladder was not a ladder as we
know the word to be used today. The original
Hebrew word used was sulom, which is a
graduated incline, a.k.a. stairway; staircase.*

The Craft are
offered two overt
stairways within the
first two Blue Lodge
Degrees. The Entered
Apprentice Degree
offers the first; the
Fellow Craft the
second.

The Entered
Apprentice Degree
stairway is reflected
in the Work to which
its Ritual alludes, but
not in the Ritual work itself. The same applies to
Fellow Craft Ritual.

The Entered Apprentice Work focuses upon
bringing order to the chaos of the heart. The Fellow
Craft Work focuses upon *bringing order to the chaos
of the head (his mind).* Both are required to ensure
that a firm and strong connection exists.

You might ask in relation to the Apprentice Work,
"What is that heart connection?" and you'd be
justified in your curiosity in doing so.

Each stairway is a direct connection from Heaven.
When you don't build them, or build them well, your
connections suffer greatly. When you don't build
them and do so with due consideration of each other,

you may just find yourself pulled in two entirely different directions. If that pull is strong enough, you might just find yourself severed in twain.

Ashlars

There's a direct connection between the symbolism of the Ashlars and Jacob's Ladder. Before we address that connection, let's first lay a foundational understanding.

Freemasonic Ashlars are symbolic for living stones and more specifically they represent within Ritual the following:

> *Men who are freeborn, believe in God, are foundationally good and known as such, who have both the capacity and desire to improve themselves and have shown that they have done some improvement Work already.*

Please recall that within Stonecraft an ashlar is freeborn (as in: suitable, superior and excellent stock; alluding to the qualities of freestone). They are also claimed by someone, show no flaws that would prevent them from being used appropriately by a Builder and they're hewn to some degree.

Most stones are bound as aggregate within the earth. Some of these stones get free. Some of those freed stones, but only those that are excellent, wind up being hewn into shape through specific and directed Work to become useful to the builder.

Masons then shape them for building purposes.

Let's review all this on purpose.

The use of Ashlars within Ritual is to point out through metaphor and through allegory that men who desire more must qualify (be suitable) to become members. Additionally, they must aspire *through their actions* to become both better and a part of something bigger, grander and important *to God*.

Jacob's Ladder

This theological *sulom* both represents and is a symbolic connection between heaven and earth. Through the story of Jacob, it is revealed that it was created and it was provided by God to mankind. It is a means by which angels (God's Messengers) descend and ascend between the two.

Should a man desire to strengthen this connection, and more specifically his connection, between Heaven and Earth and to have better communication between himself and God, Ritual tells and shows him that there is specific Work to which it directs him to do by way of its use.

Once again, let's review all this on purpose.

The ladder's intent within Ritual is to point out metaphorically and allegorically that there's both a connection and there is Work that men must do to strengthen that connection.

There's a caveat in this though. *The Work strengthens this connection only and does not guarantee anything more.* It is entirely upon the shoulders of the individual doing the Work to make that personal connection Strong.

Relationship

Symbolically, you're the Ashlar (below) and the Ladder (stairway) is a connection between what exists Above (God) with that which exists Below (God's Creation).

Both the Ladder and its connection allude to the Work that improves your connection between:

1. Heaven and Earth
2. The Almighty and You

When you desire to *perfect* the connection between yourself and God, Work your Ashlar toward being suitable to the situation!

Back to Center

Let's bring this back to the whole focus of this writing. The use of the word *perfect* here is in the verb form – it is action-based. The intended meaning conveyed by it is *"to bring nearer to perfection; improve; make better"* which is right in line with the Craft's stated goal: *To make good men better!*

Should you care to explore the word *perfection*, you'll quickly find it means: *the highest degree of proficiency, skill, or excellence, as in some art.*

Proficiencies are not just about memorizing and repeating back what one is told. Proficiencies are about Work that brings about skill and excellence from the men who undergo it with the strict intent *to improve men from good to better.*

This is the whole purpose of what the Craft should be focusing upon with its Candidates and members. This, at least, is what Ritual points us toward continuously.

Perfect Levels

From all that has been offered up through this presented research, it should be clear by now that the word *perfect* has had a variety of meanings assigned to it over the years. Each provides its own meaning through the context surrounding it. When that context is Freemasonic in nature, we cannot take for granted that the intended meaning is one based upon mainstream use and not one that is now obsolete. When we dismiss meanings long retired from profane use, we risk losing important and crucial Masonic Light that is interwoven for our benefit.

Research shows us that ritual use of the word *perfect* falls into several categories, some are archaic and obsolete. When we apply these obsolete and archaic meanings suitably and maturely to the context of the text surrounding these words, rather than assuming these words have the same meanings used within common society, the meanings of each conveyance become different, redirected and more aligned with the purpose of Freemasonry.

Equally important to these conveyed meanings are the applications to which such meanings allude. Selecting appropriate meanings based upon context are more apt to produce long term motivational success than far-reaching scopes. The differences between mastering a catechism and mastering the use of grammar are many. While the first requires proper pronunciation, timing and memory recall, the latter requires an in-depth understanding of language mechanics. Each mastered skill is commendable unto itself and each requires its own investments.

The same goes for every Masonic development opportunity offered up by Freemasonic ritual.

Opportunities

The Organization offers a variety of opportunities for Mastery to be achieved. Taking on roles within Degrees, an officer or lodge support person are some

opportunities. Playing member support roles such as trainer, mentor, instructor or coach are others. Playing an intricate part in your personal development or that of another are also key roles to take on.

No matter what the direction you choose to take, *perfecting* each role so that it plays out Masterfully is key. And while Mastery of every role is not likely to occur, should you choose to specialize and refine your skills so that you stand out well and for all the right reasons, perfecting a single role is highly probable when you invest yourself in that direction.

The key is to not allow unrealistic expectations, unsuitable definitions or grossly misinformed attitudes to lead you astray. You're likely to perfect whatever role you wish to wear, within the Craft or without, when you invest in mastering all that it takes to bring that role into a shining example of what can be accomplished when you invest yourself.

Keep in mind the underlying goal of Masonry. It is to make good men better.

In other words: *To Perfect Men*
May your efforts be perfect!

Points to Perpend:

1) How are you going about strengthening your Stairway?
2) What perfecting activities have you engaged in so far to do that strengthening?
3) What *more can you do?*

Appendix

A. Some Perfect Checklists

The Moral Integrity Checklist:

1. Find & Interview trusted Brothers who have successfully done this Work to assist in your efforts.
2. Create an Advisory Board to assist you.
3. Create an appropriate Moral Integrity Assessment.*
4. Honestly assess your Moral Integrity: Match your Professed Word with your Observed Action.*
5. Create your action plan to improve your Moral Integrity performance with timelines & milestones.*
6. Commit to and Implement your plan.
7. Meet with your Advisory Board on a regular basis and adjust your actions accordingly.

The Vice & Superfluity Checklist:

1. Find & Interview trusted Brothers who have done this Work successfully.
2. Create an Advisory Board to assist you.
3. Figure out for yourself what Vices & Superfluities truly are and create an appropriate Assessment.*
4. Honestly assess your Vices & Superfluities: Identify your most obvious Vices & Superfluities.*
5. Create your Vices & Superfluities Divestment action plan with timelines & milestones.*
6. Commit to & Implement your plan.
7. Meet with your Advisory Board on a regular basis and adjust your actions accordingly.

The Passions & Desires Checklist:

1. Find & Interview trusted Brothers who have done this Work successfully.
2. Create an Advisory Board to assist you.
3. Create an appropriate Passions & Desires Assessment.*
4. Honestly assess your Passions & Desires: Identify your Circumscribe & Subdue Successes & Failures.*
5. Create your action plan to improve your Circumscribe & Subdue performance with timelines & milestones.*
6. Commit to and Implement your plan.
7. Meet with your Advisory Board on a regular basis and adjust your actions accordingly.

The Twenty-Four Inch Gauge Checklist:

1. Find & Interview trusted Brothers who have done this Work successfully.
2. Create an Advisory Board to assist you.
3. Create an appropriate Time Management Abilities assessment.*
4. Honestly assess your Time Management Abilities: Identify where you do well and where you fail.*
5. Create your action plan to improve your Time Management Abilities with timelines & milestones.*
6. Commit to & Implement your plan.
7. Meet with your Advisory Board on a regular basis and adjust your actions accordingly.

Validate this! Get feedback and reality checks from your Advisory Board!

B. A General Assessment

The premise of passing Apprentices to Fellow Crafts is that rough ashlars have been properly worked to produce suitable perfect ashlars.

Without a doubt, to progress in masonry you must uncover and apply its hidden and vital truths toward perfecting ashlars and then apply these truths to your every day practices. Performing such actions requires dedication and persistence that not many brothers possess. When you work at it diligently, you eventually uncover hidden and vital truths about yourself, and in doing so, you also discover your hidden and vital self.

The First Degree Ritual is rich with allusions to the Work-men must do to move themselves from youth (*immaturity*) to adulthood (*maturity*). Examining the First Degree in depth reveals specific self-disclosing tasks that enable this maturing process through to fruition. Such engagements transform rough ashlars to common ashlars and, if continued, eventually transform it into a passable perfect ashlar.

Maturing younger members of the Craft is written within our code. It is the movement from the first step to the second. To ignore this activity is to advance members detrimentally to themselves and to the whole of the fraternity.

How to Know

How do I know when I have completed the Apprentice Work?

This is an extremely useful question to ask, especially when you are actively seeking to move from apprentice to fellow craft as directed by Ritual.

Out of all the topics that are confusing in the minds of far too many brothers, this is one of the top ten.

There exists a huge swath of members who are of the mentality that, because one can never be *flawless, one is always an apprentice.* As denoted by the chapters within this writing, this is a misleading conclusion that is wrought by the wrongful application of a non-Freemasonic doctrine that they have brought with them when they joined and then applied upon the existing dogma of the Fraternity.

Above all, Apprentice work is about laying a foundation. It is about preparing to build and learn. It is not about being flawless and it never was! It is about building a strong foundation of maturity.

Provided herein are categories of maturity alluded to within Freemasonic Ritual that contain four statements having to do with the most rudimentary aspects of each. Assess yourself using the provided key contained in the scoring section at the end of this assessment.

Once you assess yourself, review the **Points to Perpend** section to ascertain what actions you can take to improve your score.

How do you see your Masonic development progressing using this very rudimentary assessment,

as Preston-Webb based rituals allude and instruct us?
Assess yourself and find out!

Let's go through the list!

1. Proactive

This takes into account self-prompting into engaging actions that you know you need to take to deal with life as a self-starter. You have trained yourself to be self-initiating. You do not wait for others to prompt you toward taking actions that you know need to be taken. You see what needs to be done and you initiate work in that direction without being prompted by others to get started.

1. I continuously ask myself, "What's next?"
2. I take the time to look at what I want to accomplish next.
3. I imagine what I should be taking action on and do so without external prompting.
4. I take the initiative on what I want to accomplish.

2. Integrity

This is when your thoughts, words and actions are all in accord with each other. You know where you have integrity and where you lack integrity.

1. My thoughts, words and actions do not contradict one other.
2. When I give my word, others can depend upon it being realized as stated.
3. I am acutely aware when I am out of integrity and take action to get back into integrity.

4. I am acutely aware when others are out of integrity and place appropriate value upon them thereafter.

3. Impulse Control

This is where you show tremendous restraint while facing conditions and situations where you might easily react without thinking through your options fully and with due consideration. You're temperate in your choices, decisions and actions. You're never rushing into any situations, reacting or engaging without first thinking things through.

1. I pause to consider possible outcomes before I make my next move.
2. I take the necessary time to discern what my choices and decisions might bring about.
3. I consider the long term consequences of what I am about to do or not do..
4. I respond appropriately to what is before me, rather than react without thoughtfulness.

4. Self-knowledge

This requires that you know yourself very well and, because you do, you come to know others very well too, sometimes even better than they may know themselves. You are not in denial about who you truly are and what you do.

1. I know myself; the good, the bad and the ugly.
2. I am aware when what I know about myself is not how I want to see myself.

3. I continually take what I know about myself into consideration when faced with situations and people that ask me to change.
4. I am unwilling to change myself for the worse when faced with challenges to my integrity.

5. Important/Unimportant

Before you can set your priorities, you have to first understand and then come to know and ultimately recognize that which nurtures/depletes yourself and others. You know what's important to you and what is not.

1. I take the time to discern and establish firmly what and who is important and unimportant to me.
2. I recognize what and who is important and unimportant to me.
3. I understand what and who is important and unimportant to me.
4. My behavior consistently honors and supports what and who is important to me.

6. Priorities

These are choices and decisions supportive of what's professed, but more typically shown through actions, to be most important. You focus on things that are important. You do not participate long or frequently in any activities that are unimportant.

1. I know what my priorities are.
2. I understand what my priorities are.

3. My behavior consistently honors and supports my priorities.
4. I do not associate long with those who make efforts to change my priorities to my detriment.

7. Judgment

This is the effort you put into your choices and decisions that make for the best possible outcomes. This includes seeking the advice and life experiences of others when you have yet to experience what you have before you. You are prudent in your choices, decisions, and actions, thinking through situations and considering what best outcomes could be initiated.

1. I seek the best possible outcomes.
2. I do not guess when I know or believe a better choice is possible.
3. I know and admit when I do not have the wisdom to deal with a situation.
4. I seek advice and the experience others have to offer me. '

8. Critical Thinking

This requires that you have the capacity to think through things critically, never assuming any offered information, suggestion or advice is true or false or relevant to the situation. You take time to examine things in depth and do not get distracted by superficial impressions.

1. I do not assume things are as they appear to be.
2. I consider the possibility that what is actually offered is not as presented.

3. I engage in activities scrutinizing what might be assumed to be correct.
4. I look beyond what is before me and into the premises upon which they are founded.

9. Choices & Decisions

This requires that you know what you want, what you do not want and what you are willing to let go of to get what you want. You make better, and more importantly, *more mature* choices & decisions because you know what is important and what is not.

1. My choices and decisions are founded upon a firm understanding of what is important and unimportant to me.
2. I know that a choice is based upon what I want and that a decision requires that I let go of something when required to  make a selection which eliminates at least one possibility.
3. I can deal with the loss of possibility appropriately.
4. I know what I want and recognize when a possibility is inappropriate to the desired end.

10. Values

This is what you regard highly and that is something to be held as deserving. You believe it to be of importance, worth, or usefulness. This includes ideals. You know what you value, and what you don't value and why. You do not profess or claim false values.

1. I know what my values are.
2. I understand the basis of my values.
3. I evaluate my behaviors in both typical and atypical situations to ensure that they honor my values.
4. My behaviors honor and support my values.

11. Improvement

This is what you know that adds value to who you are and what you do. You know what betterment means to you and for you and you have focused your energies upon bringing this about and do so without excuse.

1. I know what creates greater value.
2. I understand the basis for adding value.
3. My improvement efforts are based upon adding value.
4. My improvement efforts are in alignment with what I profess to value.

12. Beliefs

These are either your acceptance that a statement is true or that something exists. You know what you have chosen to believe and why.

1. I know what I believe.
2. I understand what I believe.
3. My beliefs honor and support my values.
4. My behavior honors and supports my beliefs

13. Morality

These are behaviors that honor and support one's values and beliefs. Most often these shall be found in some sort of sacred text or scriptures, but morals are not limited to these writings and can be found anywhere there are examples of human interaction written, spoken or acted out. They agree with beliefs and values and they strengthen, support and protect the individual's self-interests. You know your morals and can express them clearly and succinctly. What's more, you know where you are immoral, the consequences of that immorality and willingly embrace the liabilities involved and without excuse.

1. I know what my morals are.
2. I understand what my morals are.
3. My morals honor and support what is and who are important to me.
4. I do not associate long with those who dishonor or don't support my morals.

14. Standards

These are your personal windows of operation. They are your limits for which you hold yourself to account. You have established specific standards to which you make every effort to live authentically and without excuse.

1. I know what my standards are.
2. I understand the basis behind my standards.
3. My behavior supports and honors my standards.
4. I do not associate long with those who make efforts to have me dishonor or disrespect my standards.

15. Emotions (Passions and Desires)

These are the patterns of your body energy which are a direct result of how you perceive situations, things, and people and engage yourself with them. You fully understand the difference between desires and passions and ensure that you circumscribe and subdue them accordingly.

1. I know what each of my emotions says to me about how I perceive the world, when they occur.
2. I understand the message behind each emotion as they occur.
3. I take appropriate and mature actions when I am aware of any specific emotion in myself or another.
4. I know how to subdue my passions, I do so when necessary and I circumscribe my desires appropriately whenever they occur.

16. Subduing

This requires an in-depth understanding of what you want and how to direct yourself in ways that are considerate and respectful of all involved. You know what your desires are and employ successful methods that keep them subdued.

1. I know what drives my desires and recognize when they are misdirected.
2. I do not deny my desires; I make sure they are addressed appropriately.
3. I do not suppress my desires; I direct them appropriately.
4. I ensure that my desires are appropriate to the situation and direct them according to what is acceptable.

17. Boundaries

These are your social windows of operation. They are the limits for which you hold others to account. You successfully both establish and maintain your boundaries as needed and appropriate to others.

1. I know what my boundaries are.
2. I understand the basis behind my boundaries.
3. My behavior supports and honors my boundaries.
4. I do not associate long with those who dishonor or disrespect my boundaries.

18. Circumscription

This requires you to understand and direct what you would willingly suffer for such that it doesn't require others to suffer as well. You know what your passions are and you employ successful methods that keep them circumscribed.

1. I understand what I am willing to suffer to get what I want.

2. I ensure that my actions to get what I want do not require others to suffer.
3. I demand that my suffering should never require others to suffer as well.
4. I stay within acceptable limits to ensure that the suffering I willingly endure is not visited upon others.

19. Ethics

These are behaviors that honor and support groups. They are mutually agreed upon and mutually supported under the premise that they strengthen, support and protect the group. You are aware of the standards of any group you belong to and adhere to them respectfully.

1. I know what my group ethics are
2. I understand why I adhere to the group ethics I profess to hold.
3. My behavior honors and supports my group's ethics.
4. I do not associate long with those who make efforts to have me dishonor or disrespect my group's ethics.

20. Civility

This ensures that you respect others without compromising your own principles and beliefs. You integrate your knowledge, morality, awareness and skill sets effectively and considerately into all your daily dealings with others.

1. I remain steadfast in my respect for others even when in disagreement or at odds.
2. I take no actions that would be inconsiderate of others.
3. I engage in activities with others that show respect and consideration.
4. When faced with a no-win situation, I take the path that indicates the most respect and consideration for everyone involved.

21. Vision

This requires you to think ahead, imagining what the future could be for what you wish to accomplish. You have developed and embraced a clear vision as to what you need to do to mature.

1. My visions are based upon what I truly want to accomplish.
2. I actively engage in the practice of visualizing what the future could be.
3. I seek to imagine different scenarios where what I want to occur comes into being.
4. I engage my imagination toward solutions to ensure that what I imagine is not sabotaged/prevented.

22. Planning

This requires that you keep aligned with what you want to accomplish aligned with your available resources, clearly denoting the steps you must take to reach your goals. You have taken your vision of your future and have put together a clear instruction set to ensure that you increase the probability of it unfolding as you imagine.

1. I actively engage in planning what I want to accomplish.
2. I have contingencies in place to ensure that my plans are accomplished when things occur that are beyond my control.
3. My plans are based upon sound principles.
4. When required, I adjust my plans to ensure that they are in harmony with what life affords me.

23. Organizing

This requires you to invest time to ensure that what you have is structured beneficially toward your desired ends. You invest in activities that bring order to chaos, ensuring that what you have ordered is in line with your aims.

1. I take stock of what is before me and ensure that it is ordered in beneficial ways.
2. I intentionally order my resources to align them with my goals.
3. I consider the possibility that what I have organized could be improved upon.
4. I am open to suggestions and recommendations to improve what I have organized.

24. Time management

These are the systems you employ that help you responsibly manage your time effectively and efficiently. You use time more effectively first and then you use time more efficiently next.

1. I use a time management system that supports and honors my priorities.

2. I only participate in activities that are important to me and those I care for most.
3. I do not get distracted by unimportant things, situations, and people.
4. I have systems in place to effectively handle things, situations and people that are unimportant.

25. Divestment

These are the vices and superfluities to which you applied your Common Gavel. They represent your successful removal of the unnecessary excesses in your life that would have burdened you had you not divested yourself of them. You have become skilled in both a) identifying superfluities & vices, and b) successfully divesting yourself of them once identified

1. I know what my vices and superfluities are.
2. I understand the personal basis of supporting each of them.
3. I have put in place systems that effectively deal with any vice or superfluity that might occur for me and those who might offer them to me.
4. I do not associate long with anyone who makes effort to have me participate in any vice or superfluity.

26. Investment

These are the virtues to which you have invested time to cultivate. They are disciplines and ideals that strengthen you in what you do. You make every effort to practice virtues and you have integrated them into your daily manners.

1. I know the seven virtues disclosed within the First Degree Ritual.
2. I understand how each strengthens me through its applied practice.
3. I effectively apply these virtues in all of my daily activities.
4. I see clearly what others do and I do not support or honor those individuals who clearly are not virtuous in their activities.

27. Responsibility

These are the tasks that you take upon yourself either by choice or design. You embrace responsibility for what you know you need to be doing to mature and maintain maturity.

1. I know the difference between responsibility and accountability.
2. I accept responsibility for those things that I know I can accomplish, control or direct.
3. When I am responsible for things that I know I cannot handle, I seek assistance that ensures that they are properly taken care of.
4. I appropriately notify others when my responsibility can no longer be handled by me.

28. Accountability

This is the systemic accounting of your liabilities for which you shall be held to account. You stand by, willingly embrace, and have trained yourself not to outrun by excuse authentic liabilities wrought by your choices and decisions.

1. I am rigorously honest and patiently thorough in my daily self-reflection.
2. I hold myself accountable for outcomes and results which are in my charge.
3. I systematically engage in a personal review of my responsibilities to ensure that they are being properly attended to.
4. I empower others to help me hold myself accountable and I report results to them in a timely manner to help me review them.

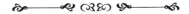

Apprentice General Assessment Scoring – *Use this form to keep track of and tally your responses using the following key:*

1) never 2) rarely 3) sometimes 4) mostly 5) always

Points to Perpend:

1. For any statement that you scored yourself less than a five on, what's missing that prevents it from being rated as a five?
2. How do you think others might score you on any listed statement and why?
3. What can you do to improve your future score?
4. In making an effort to improve yourself toward suitability, is it more important to seek flawlessness or maturity?
5. Why do you think some of the assessment statements appear to be redundant?

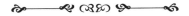

174

An Acid Test (A Mentoring & Coaching Tool):

When you want to know if Brothers are either doing or have done the Apprentice Work, just go through the above list and evaluate their progress. Are they still struggling with any of these items? *It should become evident to you by their manner, self-knowledge, and personal discipline whether they are doing or have done the work.*

My Personal Short Cut Acid Test:

I involve Brothers in conversations about whether they are still Apprentices or not. *The moment they drift into the "we're all apprentices" territory,* it's pretty clear to me that they are and very likely have no clue what the actual Apprentice Work is and what it is *intended to do* for those who do it. With such persons, *discussing or using such an assessment list at all would be a superfluous act.*

Some Final Thoughts:

Will you do all this flawlessly? There is a high probability that you will not. But *flawless perfection* was never truly the goal. The goal was to...

1. Lay the foundation, and
2. Put these activities on auto-pilot

...so that you can *continue to mature in other directions!*

C. Operative Glossary

Ashlar: 1. Stone produced for construction purposes having edges with more or less right angles, making it easier to stack. It comes in a variety of sizes.[55] 2. A stone façade of generally square or rectangular units having sawed or dressed beds.[56]

Astler: Old term for **ashlar**.[57]

Bastard Ashlar or Bastard Masonry: 1. Ashlar stones roughly dressed at the quarry and not finished. 2. Masonry material in thin stone/blocks that is square-hewn and placed to resemble ashlar.[58]

Bench: Steps formed in a quarry by removal of stone following bed joints. Or, a long seat of *cubic stone.*[59]

Broach: 1. To drill or cut out material left between closely spaced drill holes. 2. A mason's sharp-pointed chisel for dressing stone. 3. An inclined piece of masonry filling the triangular space between the base of an octagonal spire and the top of a square tower. 4. A type of chisel used for working narrow surfaces.[60]

Building Stone: Rock material in its natural state of composition and aggregation as it exists in the quarry and is usable in construction as dimension building stone. Also used interchangeably with the term, *"dimension stone."* [61]

Cubic (adjective): 1. Having three dimensions; solid. 2. Having the form of a cube; cubical. 3. Pertaining to the measurement of volume: the cubic contents of a vessel. 4. Pertaining to a unit of linear measure that is multiplied by itself twice to form a unit of measure for volume: cubic foot; cubic centimeter; cubic inch; cubic meter. **5. [Mathematics] Of or relating to the Third Degree.** 6. [Crystallography] Belonging or pertaining to the isometric system of crystallization. 7. (noun) [Mathematics] A cubic polynomial or equation.[62]

Cut Stone: Finished, dimensional stone, ready to set in place.[63]

Dimension Stone: A natural stone or rock that has been selected and finished (i.e., trimmed, cut, drilled, ground, or other) to specific sizes or shapes.[64]

Dressing: The shaping and squaring of natural stone blocks for storage and shipment. Sometimes called *scabbing.* [65]

Freestone: Superior or excellent stone; stone that may be cut freely in any direction without fracture or splitting. Also called *universal stone.* See *isotropic.*[66]

Make Ready: The act or process of making something ready for use[67]

Mantel: The structural member spanning the opening of a fireplace. Also, a shelf (usually *cubic stone*) which is part of the finish and above the fireplace opening.[68]

Quarry Block: Generally, a piece of rough stone as it comes from a quarry, generally dressed or wire sawed to the shape of a rectangular prism (having three pairs of roughly parallel faces) for shipment.[69]

Smooth Finish: A finish of minimum textural quality, presenting the least interruption of the surface. Smooth finish may be applied to any surface, flat or molded. It is produced by a variety of machines.[70]

Stone: Sometimes synonymous with rock, but more properly applied to individual blocks, masses or fragments taken from their original formation or considered for commercial use. In commercial use, the term stone is more frequently used, while scientifically, geologists and petrographers more frequently use the term rock.[71]

Thin Stone/Blocks: Dimension stone units that are 2" (50mm) or less in thickness. [72]Also referred to as, *"bastard ashlar"*.

---

[1] Joseph Joubert Pensées (1842) Sect. 21 Part 15

[2] Ludwig Wittgenstein "The Blue Book in The Blue and Brown Books, Harper and Row, New York (1958) at 67.

[3] A Nice Knock-Down Argument
by Peter Williams (after Lewis Carroll's 'Through the Looking Glass')

[4] This date is based upon the April 15, 1755 publication of Samuel Johnson's "A Dictionary of the English Language" which established the demarcation between obsolete and archaic.

[5] Captured meanings based upon period sentimentalities

[6] Gage (Noun) a valued object deposited as a guarantee of good faith.

[7] Quarried stone of excellent or superior quality with no flaws preventing it from being used for the builder's use.

[8] http://www.etymonline.com/index.php?term=ashlar

[9] http://www.dictionary.com/browse/ashlar

[10] Page 290, Ars Quatuor Coronatorum, Volume XXIX (1916)

[11] This explanation is rarely understood. Most interpret it to mean the fellow crafts do the adjusting. Nothing could be further from the truth. Since the Apprentice Work develops and hence internalizes the Fellow Craft tools, it is the Apprentice Work that actually "adjusts" aka "improves", the Perfect Ashlar.

[12] Edinburgh Register House MS 1696

[13] The Chetwode Crawley Manuscript (1700)

[14] The Sloane No.3329 Manuscript (1700)

[15] The Kevan Manuscript (1714)

[16] The Grand Mystery (1724)

[17] The Wilkinson Manuscript (1727)

[18] Masonry Dissected (1730)

[19] Catechisme Des Francs-Maçons, Page 52 (1745)

[20] Preston, William; The Lecture in the First Degree

[21] http://www.marble-institute.com/default/assets/File/consumers/glossary.pdf

[22] http://www.selectstone.com/architectural-resources/stone-glossary/

[23] http://www.selectstone.com/architectural-resources/stone-glossary/

[24] Page 34. Stone work: Designing with Stone. Malcome Holzman 2001

[25] Practical Masonry: Or A Theoretical and Operative Treatise of Building; Edward Shaw, Architect; 1846.

[26] Page 133; ibid

[27] Page 134; ibid

[28] Morgan v Jones (1773) Lofft 176; 98 ER 587 at 596 referring to John Locke's Essay on Human Understanding particularly Chs 9, 10 and 11.

[29] Confirmation bias is the tendency to search for, interpret, favor, and recall information in a way that confirms one's preexisting beliefs or hypotheses. It is a type of cognitive bias and a systematic error of inductive reasoning.

[30] (obsolete) Separate; distinct. [origin] late Middle English: from Old French, from Latin secretus (adjective) 'separate, set apart,' from the verb secernere, from se- 'apart' + cernere 'sift.'

[31] belonging exclusively to. {origin] late Middle English (in the sense 'particular'): from Latin peculiaris 'of private property', from peculium 'property', from pecu 'cattle' (cattle being private property). The sense 'strange' dates from the early 17th century.

[32] The Freemason's Treasury, 52 short lectures on the theory and practice of symbolic masonry; George Oliver (1863) page 24.

[33] The Freemason's Treasury, pages 90-91

[34] The Freemason's Treasury, Page 190-191

[35] Cymbeline; Act III Scene I Lines 70 -74

[36] https://www.etymonline.com/word/knowledgeable

[37] "The FIFTH CLAUSE", from "*A Lecture On The Various - Rituals Of Freemasonry From The Tenth Century*", Delivered in the Witham Lodge, Lincoln, 1863, by The Rev. G. Oliver, D.D.

[38] In Colin Dyer's book, *William Preston and His Work*, the author states that the first word, compiler of Preston's Lecture of the First Degree, was really "Off", not "Of". The Off referred to the fact that First Degree Candidates' clothes were removed while in the preparation room. This still remains consistent with the concept of "Preparation, Entrance, and Obligation".

[39] flawless; satisfying all requirements: accurate; corresponding to an ideal standard or abstract concept; faithfully reproducing the original specifically; legally valid; expert, proficient; pure, total; lacking in no essential detail: complete; sane; absolute; of an extreme kind; mature; certain, sure; contented, satisfied

[40] ibid

[41] "In the U.S., a person must be at least 35 years of age to be President or Vice President, 30 years to be a senator, or 25 years

to be a representative, as specified in the U.S. Constitution. Most states in the U.S. also have age requirements for the offices of governor, state senator, and state representative." Source: http://definitions.uslegal.com/a/age-of-candidacy/

[42] if one depended upon strictly upon behavior observation

[43] De Luca, Cinzia R.; Leventer, Richard J. (2008). "Developmental trajectories of executive functions across the lifespan". In Anderson, Peter; Anderson, Vicki; Jacobs, Rani (eds.). Executive functions and the frontal lobes: a lifespan perspective. Washington, DC: Taylor & Francis. pp. 24–47.

[44] http://www.hhs.gov/opa/familylife/tech_assistance/etraining/adolescent_brain/Development/prefrontal_cortex/

[45] Short Talk Bulletin - Vol. IX July, 1931 No.7

[46] Short Talk Bulletin - April 1979

[47] fit (v.) "be suitable," probably from early 15c.; "to be the right shape," 1580s, from fit (adj.). Related: Fitted; fitting. Fitted sheets is attested from 1963.
fit (adj.) "suited to the circumstances, proper," mid-15c., of unknown origin, perhaps from M.E. noun fit "an adversary of equal power" (mid-13c.), which is perhaps connected to fit (n.1). Survival of the fittest (1867) coined by H. Spencer.

[48] (Hebrew) תמים tamiym taw-meem', תם tam tawm, תמם tamam taw-mam', שלם shalem shaw-lame', שלול shalowm shaw-lome' or שלם shalom shaw-lome', הלכמ miklah mik-law', רמג gamar gaw-mar', תילכת takliyth tak-leeth', לילכ kaliyl kaw-leel', ללכ kalal kaw-lal', רמג g@mar (Aramaic) ghem-ar', (Greek) τελειος teleios tel'-i-os, τελειοω teleioo tel-i-o'-o, ακριβεια akribeia ak-ree'-bi-ah, ακριβηστερον akribesteron ak-ree-bes'-ter-on, ακριβως akribos ak-ree-boce', καταρτιζω katartizo kat-ar-tid'-zo, ολοκληρια holokleria hol-ok-lay-ree'-ah, τελειοω teleioo tel-i-o'-o, επιτελεω epiteleo ep-ee-tel-eh'-o

[49] Chapter IV: Acceptable Admittance; Building Free Men

[50] At the construction site of a cathedral, two workers were asked about the wall that they were building. One replied, "a wall" while the other replied, "a house of worship".

[51] Although this Knowledge is referred to as, "Secret", a more accurate term would be "Confidential" as it is provided under the condition that the knowledge will be only shared in restricted and acceptable ways.

[52] These last two Standards are precursors to Establishing and Maintaining Boundaries.

[53] As is, "Window of Operation"

[54] http://www.mind-development.eu/ego-autonomy.html

180

[55] Dictionary of Landscape Architecture and Construction; Alan Jay Christensen; Mcgraw-Hill; 2005

[56] http://www.marble-institute.com/default/assets/File/consumers/glossary.pdf

[57] Dictionary of Landscape Architecture and Construction; Alan Jay Christensen; Mcgraw-Hill; 2005

[58] Dictionary of Landscape Architecture and Construction; Alan Jay Christensen; Mcgraw-Hill; 2005

[59] http://www.wpg.com/stone-definitions-terminology/

[60] http://www.marble-institute.com/default/assets/File/consumers/glossary.pdf

[61] http://www.marble-institute.com/default/assets/File/consumers/glossary.pdf

[62] http://www.dictionary.com/browse/cubic (Random House Dictionary, 2016.)

[63] http://www.selectstone.com/architectural-resources/stone-glossary/

[64] ASTM, C18, C119-08 Standard Terminology Relating to Dimension Stone", ASTM, 2008, p.8 ISBN 0-8031-4118-1

[65] http://www.marble-institute.com/default/assets/File/consumers/glossary.pdf

[66] http://www.marble-institute.com/default/assets/File/consumers/glossary.pdf

[67] 1820-30; noun use of verb phrase make ready (Random House Dictionary, 2016.)

[68] http://www.wpg.com/stone-definitions-terminology/

[69] http://www.marble-institute.com/default/assets/File/consumers/glossary.pdf

[70] http://www.marble-institute.com/default/assets/File/consumers/glossary.pdf

[71] http://www.marble-institute.com/default/assets/File/consumers/glossary.pdf

[72] http://www.marble-institute.com/default/assets/File/consumers/glossary.pdf

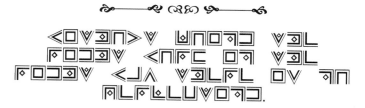